Emanations of Grace

Emanations of Grace

Mystical Poems by ^{c}Ā’ishah al-Bā^{c}ūnīyah (d. 923/1517)

Edited and Translated with an Introduction by

Th. Emil Homerin

FONS VITAE

First published in English in 2011 by
Fons Vitae
49 Mockingbird Valley Drive
Louisville, KY 40207
http://www.fonsvitae.com
Email: fonsvitaeky@aol.com

Library of Congress Control Number: 2011939594
ISBN 9781891785887

Printed in Canada

Contents

Preface

ʿĀ'ishah al-Bāʿūnīyah (d. 923/1517) was one of the greatest women scholars in Islamic history. A mystic and prolific poet and writer, ʿĀ'ishah composed more works in Arabic than any other woman prior to the 20th century. Often, she expressed her great devotion to God and His prophet Muhammad, and spoke of love and longing on the mystical quest for union. She also alluded to her extensive education and mystical training, and her own particular life experiences, which are often reflected in her verse. Her many writings were read and copied by later generations of admirers who preserved her substantial literary and mystical legacies. Though many of her works are lost today, several still exist in manuscript including her poetic collection *Fayḍ al-Faḍl wa-Jamʿ al-Shaml*: "The Emanation of Grace and the Gathering Union." The selection of poems from this volume, edited and translated into English here for the first time, recount ʿĀ'ishah al-Bāʿūnīyah's remarkable story of devotion and mystical illumination.

Acknowledgements

This study has taken shape over a number of years, and has had the support of many institutions and foundations. I am grateful for the support of the Fulbright Foundation, the National Endowment for the Humanities, and the University of Rochester. In Egypt, I was greatly assisted by Dār al-Kutub al-Miṣrīyah, the Netherlands-Flemish Institute in Cairo, the American University in Cairo, and the American Research Center in Egypt. Friends and colleagues have also graciously given me their support, and I wish to thank Daniel Beaumont, Vincent and Rkia Cornell, Kenneth Cuno, Bruce Craig, Carl Ernst, Aḥmad Ḥarīdī, Hasan al-Banna Izz al-Din, Paul Losensky, Hayat Kara, Rudolaph Peters, Carl Petry, Iymān Fu'ād Sayyid, John Swanson, and Edward Wierenga. Finally, I would like to recognize the members of my ᶜĀ'ishah al-Bāᶜūnīyah seminar, who read and discussed all of the translations with me. For their pointed questions, timely corrections, valuable insights, and, above all, their wit, and humor, I thank Rachel E. Darken, Rosemary E. Shojaie, Sarah E. Thorton, Aleeza K. Wachs, and, with love, Nora Walter.

Transliteration and Pronunciation

The transliteration of Arabic terms and verses follows the system used for Arabic by the Library of Congress. Well-known words and names, however, are generally cited in their common English forms (e.g., Sufi, not Ṣūfī; Moses, not Mūsā). When pronouncing these transliterations, the reader should be aware that Arabic vowels and consonants approximate those of English. There are three short Arabic vowels: (1) *a* as in "bat," (2) *i* as in "bit," (3) *u* as in "put," while long vowels are usually lengthened short vowels. There are two Arabic diphthongs: (1) *ay* as in the "i" of "bite," and (2) *aw* as in "cow." The majority of Arabic consonants sound like their English equivalents with the following additions: the *hamzah* (') is a glottal stop; the *ᶜayn* (ᶜ) is produced by "swallowing" the vowel immediately preceding or following it (e.g., ᶜĀ'ishah); *dh* sounds like "th"; *kh* approximates the "ch" of "loch" or "Bach; "*ḥ*" resembles a breathy, whispered "ha!" Further, there are four velarized or "emphatic" consonants: *ṣ*, *ḍ*, *ṭ*, *ẓ*, which give a "darker" quality to the surrounding vowels (e.g., Arabic *s* is pronounced like the English "sad," while *ṣ* approximates "sod."

Glossary

The glossary at the end of this book contains definitions of words whose first appearance is in *italics*, including Sufi technical terms (e.g., *Annihilation: fanā'*), various places on the Hajj pilgrimage (e.g., *Minā*), important people (e.g., *al-Jīlānī, ᶜAbd al-Qādir*), and other words and concepts essential to understanding ᶜĀ'ishah's life and work, but which may not be familiar or clear to an educated, but general audience (e.g., *Mamluk*, *Mystical Experience*, *Jinn*).

Time

All dates are cited in their Islamic/Ḥijrī year followed by their Common Era equivalent: e.g., 923/1517.

Manuscripts and Text Editions

For the Arabic text of the poems, I have relied on four manuscripts all listed under the title *Dīwān ᶜĀ'ishah al-Bāᶜūnīyah*. Three are from Cairo's Egyptian National Library: MS 431 (Shiᶜr Taymūr), dated 1031/1622; MS 581 (Shiᶜr Taymūr), dated 1031/1622, and MS 4384 (Adab), dated 1341/1922. The final manuscript is Rabat's Bibliothèque Generale #734. In 2010, the *Fayḍ al-Faḍl* was edited and published by Mahdi Asaᶜd ᶜArār. Unfortunately, his edition has many mistakes and discrepancies, and so my readings frequently differ from his. All references to ᶜĀ'ishah's verse in my introduction and the page numbers given for English translations in the anthology are to MS 431, followed by the page numbers in ᶜArār's edition. Requests for a copy of my Arabic edition of the poems in the anthology should be e-mailed to: emilhomerin@rochester.edu.

Introduction

> The sun and moon appeared on the horizon of my spirit,
>   and the heart beheld what eyes could not see,
> And sheer beauty revealed itself in guises
>   to insight's clear vision.[1]

These are the opening verses to a poem by the Muslim mystic ᶜĀ'ishah al-Bāᶜūnīyah, in which she speaks of her love for God and union with Him. Living a life of devotion, meditation, and prayer, ᶜĀ'ishah experienced moments of ecstasy marked by a sense of timeless unity and illumination:

> I behold beauty with eyes lined by His light,
>   and His splendor was the eyes' sight.
> My love's beauty is my vision, His presence my gardens,
>   and their fruit is His love talk devoted to me.[2]

Here, ᶜĀ'ishah likens her mystical state to a life of everlasting happiness in the gardens of Paradise where God will reveal Himself to those who are saved. There, too, faithful believers will drink the purest *wine*, and ᶜĀ'ishah often compares God's love to an intoxicating wine that causes her to forget herself in rapture:

> This is the tavern of joy where the glasses are full,
>   aglow like the sun and the moon.
> These choice cups are a portion of what comes to me
>   as their quiet intimacy takes hold.
> This is the wine of leisure, and I received from it
>   perfect fulfillment from an endless source,
> A wine taking me to the fountain of bliss,
>   as I attained peace without anxiety or fear.[3]

ᶜĀ'ishah's *mystical experiences* enabled her to pass away from a life of selfishness in order to see the divine within her *heart* and so live an enlightened life of love:

---

1. ᶜĀ'ishah al-Bāᶜūnīyah, *Dīwān ᶜĀ'ishah al-Bāᶜūnīyah* (= *Fayḍ al-Faḍl*), Cairo: Dār al-Kutub al-Miṣrīyah, microfilm 29322 of MS 431 (Shiᶜr Taymūr), 264, and *Dīwān Fayḍ al-Faḍl wa-Jam ᶜ al-Shaml*, edited by Mahdi As'ad ᶜArrar (Beirut, 2010), 377. See the anthology for the complete poem.
2. Ibid. 264/378.
3. Ibid., 265/378.

My mind, my spirit, my faith—all of me
 sees clearly without a veil or screen.
So I received the greatest joy and wish,
 and grace to me is limitless![4]

As ᶜĀ'ishah's spiritual life progressed, she became a *Sufi* master in her own right, and she composed a guidebook to lead others on the mystic path. Following a centuries old Sufi tradition, ᶜĀ'ishah advises the seeker to repent of selfish ways and turn to a sincere life of love for God and all of His creation. Essential to this transformation is meditation on human limitations and God's limitless love. In her poems and other writings, ᶜĀ'ishah often recounts her own *states* and *stages* on this quest for *union* with the hope that others, too, might receive an emanation of grace.

Life

ᶜĀ'ishah al-Bāᶜūnīyah was born in the 9th/15th century into a family of respected religious scholars and poets. Originating in the village of Bāᶜūn in Southern Syria, members of the Bāᶜūnī family eventually moved to Damascus. For several generations, they served the *Mamluk* sultans of Egypt and Syria, holding a number of important religious and legal positions throughout the empire. ᶜĀ'ishah's father Yūsuf (805-80/1402-1475) was a scholar of Shāfiᶜī jurisprudence and considered one of the most educated and honest judges of his day, especially in Damascus where he rose to become chief judge. He also looked after the education of his children, and so ᶜĀ'ishah and her five brothers studied the *Qur'ān*, the traditions of the prophet *Muhammad* (*ḥadīth*), jurisprudence, and poetry.[5]

While her brothers became scholars in their own right, ᶜĀ'ishah surpassed them in talent, erudition, and fame. Several contemporaries left accounts of her, including the historians Muhammad Ibn Ṭūlūn (d. 935/1529) of Damascus, and Muhammad ibn Ibrāhīm Ibn al-Ḥanbalī (d. 971/1563) of Aleppo. Drawing extensively from both sources are later notices by Muhammad al-Ghazzī (d. 1061/1651), and ᶜAbd al-Ḥayy Ibn al-ᶜImād (d. 1089/1679).[6] Un-

4. Ibid.

5. This account of the life and work of ᶜĀ'ishah al-Bāᶜūnīyah is drawn from Th. Emil Homerin, "Living Love: The Mystical Writings of ᶜĀ'ishah al-Bāᶜūnīyah," *Mamlūk Studies Review* 7:1 (2003): 211-36, with additional notes to new findings. For more on the Bāᶜūnī family see Muhammad ᶜAbd Allāh al-Qadḥāt, *ᶜĀ'ilat al-Bāᶜūnī* (Amman, 2007).

6. Ibn Ṭūlūn, *al-Qalā'id al-Jawharīyah fī Ta'rīkh a-Ṣāliḥīyah* (Damascus, 1980), 2:531, and his *Mufākahat al-Khillān fī Ḥawādith al-Zamān* (Cairo, 1962), 2:74; Ibn Mullā al-Ḥaṣkafī, *Mutᶜat al-Adhān Min al-Tamattuᶜ bi-al-Iqrān* (Beirut, 1999), 2:878-79; Ibn al-Ḥanbalī al-Ḥalabī, *Durr al-Ḥabab fī Ta'rīkh Aᶜyān Ḥalab* (Damascus, 1973), 1:2:1060-69; Najm al-Dīn Muhammad al-Ghazzī, *al-Kawākib*

fortunately, none of them cited ᶜĀ'ishah's date of birth, though Ibn Ṭūlūn, who knew her, quoted verses that ᶜĀ'ishah recited to her uncle Ibrāhīm, who died in 870/1464.[7] ᶜĀ'ishah was probably a little girl at that time, and so born around 862/1457. That she recited poetry at a young age may have been exceptional, yet ᶜĀ'ishah was a precocious child, and in one of her writings, she noted that she had memorized the entire Qur'ān by the age of eight.[8] As a teen or young woman, ᶜĀ'ishah also went on the *Hajj* pilgrimage, probably in 880/1475 with her father and other family members, and during her time in *Mecca*, she had a vision of the prophet Muhammad:

> God, may He be praised, granted me a vision of the Messenger when I was residing in holy Mecca. An anxiety had overcome me by the will of God most high, and so I wanted to visit the holy sanctuary. It was Friday night, and I reclined on a couch on an enclosed veranda overlooking the holy *Kaᶜbah* and the sacred precinct. It so happened that one of the men there was reading a poem on the life of God's Messenger, and voices arose with blessings upon the Prophet. Then, I could not believe my eyes, for it was as if I was standing among a group of women. Someone said: "Kiss the Prophet!" and a dread came over me that made me swoon until the Prophet passed before me. Then I sought his intercession and, with a stammering tongue, I said to God's Messenger, "O my master, I ask you for *intercession*!" Then I heard him say calmly and deliberately, "I am the intercessor on the Judgment Day!"[9]

As she grew older, ᶜĀ'ishah became an adept of *Islamic mysticism*, which was important to the entire family. Her great uncle Ismāᶜīl had been a Sufi ascetic; her uncle Muhammad composed a devotional poem of over a thousand verses on the prophet Muhammad, while her uncle Ibrāhīm had been the director of a Sufi chantry in Damascus. Moreover, many members of the Bāᶜūnī family, including ᶜĀ'ishah's father, were buried in a family plot adjacent to the lodge of the Sufi guide Abū Bakr ibn Dāwūd (d. 806/1403). The Bāᶜūnī family remained devoted to this Sufi and his descendents, who were affiliated with the 'Urmawī branch of the *Qādirīyah* Sufi order. In her writings, ᶜĀ'ishah specifically praised her two spiritual masters, Jamāl

---

al-Sā'irah (Beirut, 1945), 1:287-92, and ᶜAbd al-Ḥayy Ibn al-ᶜImād, *Shadharāt al-Dhahab fī Akhbār Man Dhahab* (Cairo, 1931), 8:111-13.

7. Ibn Mullā al-Ḥaṣkafī, *Mutᶜat al-Adhān*, 2:878, and al-Ghazzī, *al-Kawākib*, 1:292.

8. Ibn al-Ḥanbalī al-Ḥalabī, *Durr al-Ḥabab*, 1:2:1060-61, and also quoted in Fāris Aḥmad al-ᶜAlāwī, *ᶜĀ'ishah al-Bāᶜūnīyah al-Dimashqīyah* (Damascus, 1994), 18-20.

9. ᶜĀ'ishah al-Bāᶜūnīyah, *al-Mawrid al-Ahnā fī al-Mawlid al-Asnā*, MS 639 (Shiᶜr Taymūr), Cairo: Dār al-Kutub al-Miṣrīyah, 104-105; also quoted in Ḥasan Rabābiᶜah, *ᶜĀ'ishah al-Bāᶜūnīyah: Shāᶜirah* (Irbid, 1997), 53.

al-Dīn Ismāʿīl al-Ḥawwārī (d. 900/1495), and his successor, Muḥyī al-Dīn Yaḥyā al-'Urmawī (fl. 9-10th/15-16th c.). ʿĀ'ishah states:

> My education and development, my spiritual *effacement* and purification, occurred by the helping hand of the sultan of the saints of his time, the crown of the pure friends of his age, the beauty of truth and religion, the venerable master, father of the spiritual axes, the *axis* of existence, Ismāʿīl al-Ḥawwārī—may God sanctify his heart and be satisfied with him—and, then, by the helping hand of his successor in spiritual states and stations, and in spiritual *proximity* and *union*, Muḥyī al-Dīn Yaḥyā al-'Urmawī—may God continue to spread his ever-growing spiritual blessings throughout his lifetime, and join us every moment to his blessings and succor.[10]

The relationship between ʿĀ'ishah and Ismāʿīl al-Ḥawwārī appears to have been particularly close, for in several of her works ʿĀ'ishah described herself as "related to Yūsuf ibn Aḥmad al-Bāʿūnī on earth, and in truth to the unique axis, Jamāl al-Dīn Ismāʿīl al-Ḥawwārī."[11] Further, after al-Ḥawwārī died in 900/1495, ʿĀ'ishah had a sarcophagus erected around his grave and a house built nearby for her so that she could place a lamp on her master's grave every Friday evening.[12]

As prominent citizens of Damascus, the Bāʿūnīs married several of their daughters to the sons of another distinguished family known as Ibn Naqīb al-Ashrāf, who were descendents of the prophet Muhammad. ʿĀ'ishah married Aḥmad ibn Muhammad Ibn Naqīb al-Ashrāf (d. 909/1503), who was also devoted to Ismāʿīl al-Ḥawwārī.[13] At the end of one of her books in praise of the prophet Muhammad, ʿĀ'ishah recorded her husband's genealogy as a descendent from Muhammad via his daughter Faṭimah and her husband ʿAlī and through their son al-Ḥusayn. She then added the name and year of birth for their own son ʿAbd al-Wahhāb (b. 897/1489), and daughter Barakah (b. 899/1491). She did this to bestow on them the blessings due to her for praising the Prophet in her book, and to certify her son's lineage as a descendent of the Prophet thereby qualifying him for a stipend in Damascus. However,

---

10. Ibn al-Ḥanbalī al-Ḥalabī, *Durr al-Habab*, 1:2:1063-64.

11. E.g. ʿĀ'ishah al-Bāʿūnīyah, *Dīwān ʿĀ'ishah al-Bāʿūnīyah* (= *Fayḍ al-Faḍl*), Cairo: Dār al-Kutub al-Miṣrīyah, microfilm 29322 of MS 431 (Shiʿr Taymūr), 2.

12. Several sources note that, late in life, Shaykh Ismāʿīl was seized by "a drying of his brain" (*nashshāf*; *jaffa dimāghuhu*) leading to his loss of reason, suggesting mental illness and/or dementia; Ibn Ṭūlūn, *al-Qalā'id*, 2:531; Ibn Mullā al-Ḥaṣkafī, *Mutʿat al-Adhān*, 1:292; al-Ghazzī, *al-Kawākib*, 1:121. Also see Josef W. Meri, *The Cult of the Saints Among Muslims and Jews in Medieval Syria* (Oxford, 2002), 170.

13. Ibn Ṭūlūn, *al-Qalā'id*, 2:531.

ᶜĀ'ishah's note also suggests that there may have been some difficulty in collecting this stipend, which probably became more important to the family after the death of ᶜĀ'ishah's husband in 909/1503.[14]

Perhaps for this reason, ᶜĀ'ishah set out for Cairo with her son in 919/1513 to secure a job for him in the Mamluk administration. Unfortunately en route, their caravan was attacked in the Egyptian delta by bandits who robbed them of everything, including all of ᶜĀ'ishah writings. When they finally arrived destitute in Cairo, ᶜĀ'ishah requested the assistance of a family friend, Maḥmūd ibn Muhammad ibn Ajā (854-925/1450-1519), the confidential secretary and foreign minister of the Mamluk sultan al-Ghawrī (r.906-922/1501-16). Ibn Ajā treated them graciously and soon employed her son in the chancery. Ibn Ajā also gave ᶜĀ'ishah an apartment in his harem next to his wife Sitt al-Ḥalab (d. 933/1526), who was the wealthy daughter of an important Mamluk amir. Sitt al-Ḥalab was on friendly terms with a wife of the sultan, the Circassian princess Jān-i Sukkar, with whom she met at monthly soirees, and perhaps ᶜĀ'ishah attended some of these sessions as well.

ᶜĀ'ishah stayed on in Cairo where she studied and shared views with a number of the finest scholars of the time. ᶜĀ'ishah continued to enjoy Ibn Ajā's patronage, for which she praised him in several panegyrics, and she also re-wrote some of her lost works, composed new ones, and exchanged a number of witty poems with fellow scholars and poets. Then, after three years, in 922/1516, ᶜĀ'ishah left Cairo with her son, ᶜAbd al-Wahhāb. He had been promoted to the position of assistant secretary and been assigned to accompany Ibn Ajā to Aleppo. There, ᶜĀ'ishah had a personal audience with the sultan al-Ghawrī, after which, she returned home to Damascus, where she died the following year in 923/1517. Our sources do not tell us why ᶜĀ'ishah met with al-Ghawrī in Aleppo, where the sultan was gathering an army for war against the Ottomans. Al-Ghawrī loved poetry, and he may have desired to hear ᶜĀ'ishah recite some of her verse. But the sultan may have met with ᶜĀ'ishah to seek her spiritual blessings, as well. For facing an imminent battle with a superior Ottoman army, al-Ghawrī was also marshaling his spiritual forces for the days and battles ahead, and it is quite apparent from biographies of ᶜĀ'ishah, that she was highly regarded as a pious woman and Sufi master by the end of her life.[15]

---

14. ᶜĀ'ishah al-Bāᶜūnīyah, *al-Mawrid al-Ahnā*, 355-56; also see Ibn al-Ḥanbalī al-Ḥalabī, *Durr al-Habab*, 1:2:1064; Rabābiᶜah, *ᶜĀ'ishah al-Bāᶜūnīyah: Shāᶜirah*, 46-47, and ᶜAbd Allāh Mukhliṣ, "ᶜĀ'ishah al-Bāᶜūnīyah," *Mujallat al-Majmaᶜ al-ᶜIlmī* 16:2:66-72 (Damascus, 1941), esp. 69.

15. Ibn Ṭūlūn, *Mufākahat*, 2:74; Th. Emil Homerin, "Writing Sufi Biography: The Case of ᶜĀ'ishah al-Bāᶜūnīyah (d. 923/1517)," *Muslim World* 96:3 (2006): 389-99, and see Carl Petry, *Twilight of Majesty* (Seattle, 1993), 224-25.

Work and Thought

ᶜĀ'ishah al-Bāᶜūnīyah was one of the most learned and prolific women scholars in all of Islamic history. While there have always been significant numbers of educated women in Muslim lands, women scholars of the premodern period seldom composed original works of their own.[16] ᶜĀ'ishah, however, was singled out by her peers for her religious prose and poetry, and she wrote more Arabic works than any other woman prior to the twentieth century. Though many of her writings are lost, we know from surviving manuscripts and from her own statements that most of her work revolved around mystical themes and the celebration of the life of Muhammad. ᶜĀ'ishah composed a number of works on Muhammad combining prose and poetry (*mawlids*), and praising the Prophet became ᶜĀ'ishah's vocation, one perhaps undertaken after her vision of him while on pilgrimage. She found such praise to be a source of strength and blessing, as she noted in the introduction to one of her long panegyrics to the Prophet:

> Praising the noble Prophet is a distinguishing feature of the pious and a sign of those who are successful. Those who desire the best, desire to praise him, while the pure of heart praise him without end, for this is among the best ways to achieve success and a means for doubling rewards![17]

ᶜĀ'ishah also copied and composed works on Sufism, and those that survive give us an idea of some of her religious influences and mystical thought. She had read and made a copy of al-Nawawī's (d. 676/1277) famous book on prayer, the *Kitāb al-Adhkār* ("The Book of Recollections"), as well as the *Kitāb al-Taᶜrīfāt* ("The Book of Definitions"), an important Sufi lexicon by al-Jurjānī (d. 816/1413). ᶜĀ'ishah also made an abridged version of a popular spiritual guidebook by ᶜAbd Allāh al-Anṣārī (d. 481/1089), the *Manāzil al-Sā'irīn* ("Stages for the Wayfarers"), and she composed her own compendium entitled *al-Muntakhab fī Uṣūl al-Rutab fī ᶜIlm al-Taṣawwuf* ("Selections on the Fundamentals of Stations in the Science of Sufism"). In this latter work, she quotes excerpts from a number of earlier Sufi masters,

---

16. See al-ᶜAlāwī, *ᶜĀ'ishah al-Bāᶜūnīyah al-Dimashqīyah*, 36-37; Huda Lutfi, "Al-Sakhawī's *Kitāb al-Nisā'* as a Source For the Social and Economic History of Muslim Women During the Fifteenth Century A.D.," *Muslim World* 71(1981):104-24, esp. 121, and Jonathan P. Berkey, "Women and Islamic Education in the Mamluk Period," in *Women in Middle Eastern History*, ed. Nikki R. Keddie and Beth Baron (New Haven, 1991), 143-57.

17. Mājid al-Dhahabī and Ṣalāḥ al-Khiyamī, "Dīwān ᶜĀ'ishah al-Bāᶜūnīyah," *Turāth al-ᶜArabī* (Damascus), 4 (1981):110-121, esp. 112, and al-ᶜAlāwī, *ᶜĀ'ishah al-Bāᶜūnīyah*, 44-47.

including al-Kalābādhī (d. 385/995), al-Sulamī (d. 412/1021), and especially, al-Qushayrī (d. 465/1074). ᶜĀ'ishah was also well versed in the writings of the founder of her order, *ᶜAbd al-Qādir al-Jīlānī* (d. 561/1166), as well as the work of ᶜUmar al-Suhrawardī (d. 632/1234) and Ibn ᶜAṭā Allāh al-Iskandarī (d. 709/1309).[18]

In her *Selections*, ᶜĀ'ishah follows in the classical Qādarīyah Sufi tradition by stressing the omnipotence of God in all affairs, while affirming that the all-powerful God is also all-merciful and forgiving. One seeking God's favor must repent (*tawbah*) and discipline the selfish *soul* (*nafs*), so that God's grace may be seen within the *heart* (*qalb/sirr*). Then, the believer can cultivate a sincere devotional life to God (*ikhlāṣ*) and serve humanity based on love (*maḥabbah*). An essential means to attain and maintain a religious life of love is *dhikr*, *recollection*. ᶜĀ'ishah quotes God's vow in the Qur'ān (2:152): "Remember Me, and I will remember you," urging the seeker to pray and remember God often.[19]

In the Sufi tradition, however, *dhikr* also refers to the practice of recollection and meditation on God, which may lead to mystical union with Him. ᶜĀ'ishah regarded *dhikr* as both a process and a mystical state. As a process, recollection of God is a way to purify oneself of selfishness and hypocrisy, and a means to keep Satan at bay. As a mystical state, recollection differs in its effects depending on the believer's spiritual level; common people are calmed and blessed by praising God, while religious scholars gain insight into Him. By contrast, recollection purifies the spiritual elect, who are absorbed and rest in God. For a powerful recollection, ᶜĀ'ishah recommends that seekers recite and meditate on the declaration of faith "There is no deity but God."[20]

In the *Selections*, ᶜĀ'ishah often cites verses from the Qur'ān and sayings from Muhammad regarding God's love of humanity and His promise to forgive the sins of those who repent. ᶜĀ'ishah urges all sincere believers to love God, His prophet Muhammad, and fellow believers. Significantly, for those graced by God, this love will eradicate selfishness and even the sense of self, as God overwhelms them with union. ᶜĀ'ishah reinforces this point with a saying popular among the Sufis, and known as the"Tradition of Willing Devotions:" "God said: 'My servant draws near to Me by nothing more loved by Me than the religious obligations that I have imposed upon

---

18. ᶜĀ'ishah al-Bāᶜūnīyah *al-Muntakhab fī Uṣūl al-Rutab fī ᶜIlm al-Taṣawwuf*, Cairo: Dār al-Kutub al-Miṣrīyah, microfilm 13123 of MS 318 (Taṣawwuf Taymūr), 1074/1663.

19. Homerin,"Living Light," 227-34.

20. ᶜĀ'ishah al-Bāᶜūnīyah *al-Muntakhab*, 102-29. For more on this *dhikr* formula see Fritz Meir, "The Dervish Dance: An Attempt at an Overview," in *Essays on Islamic Piety and Mysticism*, tr. John O'Kane (Leiden, 1999), 23-48, esp. 25-27.

him, and My servant continues to draw near to Me by acts of willing devotion such that I love him. Then, when I love him, I become his ear, his eye, and his tongue, his heart and reason, his hand and support.'"[21]

ᶜĀ'ishah adds that many people and religions of the past have tasted God's love, which is His greatest secret and an endless sea. Yet the most blessed was the prophet Muhammad and then his spiritual, saintly descendants (*awlīyā'*), especially ᶜAbd al-Qādir al-Jīlānī and Ismāᶜīl al-Ḥawwārī. God has eradicated them and all those He loves in a state beyond description, as they pass away to abide in Him. Then their hearts become a place of vision where the truth of the divine essence is revealed. As love draws seekers ever closer to their divine beloved, God bestows His love as an act of unearned grace. Ultimately, the lovers lose all sense of self when the truth of oneness appears, but their mystical death leads them to eternal life, as ᶜĀ'ishah declares in verses at the end of her *Selections*:[22]

God looked with favor on a folk,
and they stayed away from worldly fortunes.
In love and devotion, they worshipped Him;
they surrendered themselves, their aim was true.
In love with Him, they gave themselves up
and passed away from existence, nothing left behind.
So He took pity
and revealed Himself to them
And they lived again, gazing at that living face,
when His eternal life appeared.
They saw Him alone in the garden of union
and drank from contemplation's cups,
Filled lovingly with pure wine
from the vision of true oneness.

Sufi Verse

ᶜĀ'ishah included a number of original poems in her *Selections* in order to highlight her themes of repentance, sincerity, recollection, and love. But she also composed a considerable amount of other verse on Muhammad and mystical topics. To date, two collections of this verse have been found. One, entitled simply *Dīwān ᶜĀ'ishah al-Bāᶜūnīyah* ("ᶜĀ'ishah al-Bāᶜūnīyah: Collected Works"), contains six long odes in praise of the prophet Muhammad, which ᶜĀ'ishah composed during her stay in Cairo.[23] Among them is

21. Ibid, 148.
22. Ibid., 190-211, and Homerin, "Living Light," 227-34.
23. Al-Dhahabī and al-Khiyamī, "Dīwān ᶜĀ'ishah al-Bāᶜūnīyah,"112-13; this valuable article also contains a description of this collection.

an ode incorporating al-Būṣīrī's (d. 694/1295) celebrated panegyric to Muhammad, the *Burdah*, and ᶜĀ'ishah's most famous poem, the *Fatḥ al-Mubīn fī Madḥ al-Amīn* ("The Clear Inspiration in Praise of the Trusted Prophet"). The *Clear Inspiration* is a *badīᶜīyah*, a very difficult type of poem that arose during the Mamluk period, and which praises the Prophet while illustrating various rhetorical schemes (*badīᶜ*) used in Arabic verse.[24] For the *Clear Inspiration*, ᶜĀ'ishah composed 130 verses, each containing a rhetorical device (e.g. alliteration, antithesis) together with a praiseworthy attribute or action of the Prophet. ᶜĀ'ishah consciously patterned her *Clear Inspiration* on the *badīᶜīyah* poems by Ṣafī al-Dīn al-Ḥillī (d. 749/1349), and Ibn Ḥijjah al-Ḥamawī (d. 838/1434), and she further displayed her extensive knowledge of Arabic verse in a commentary to the poem in which she referred to nearly fifty earlier poets.[25]

The second collection of her verse that has survived is often incorrectly listed in manuscript collections as the *Dīwān ᶜĀ'ishah al-Bāᶜūnīyah*, though ᶜĀ'ishah herself entitled the work *Fayḍ al-Faḍl wa-Jamᶜ al-Shaml* ("The Emanation of Grace and the Gathering Union").[26] This is a remarkable autobiographical collection, which, ᶜĀ'ishah says, "contains poetry inspired by Him regarding intimate conversations with the divine and spiritual meanings, states of grace and mystical struggle, matters of desire and passionate ways."[27] In her short introduction to this work, ᶜĀ'ishah notes that she made this collection of poems "as a distraction" for one who had attained union and the favor of the prophet Muhammad, which is a likely reference to her spiritual guide, Ismāᶜīl al-Ḥawwārī.[28]

Unlike the six odes of the *Dīwān*, which ᶜĀ'ishah composed in a space of three years, the *Emanation of Grace* contains over 350 poems, which span much of her mystical life. In a note appearing mid-way through the volume, her teacher Ismāᶜīl al-Ḥawwārī described these poems as inspired works from ᶜĀ'ishah's "days as a novice and student, to her mastery of the branches of mystical *annihilation* and the arts of effacement."[29] Then,

---

24. See "*badīᶜiyyāt*," (P. Cachia), in *Encyclopedia of Arabic Literature*, ed. Julie Scott Meisami and Paul Starkey, (London, 1998), 1:124.

25. Al-Dhahabī and al-Khiyamī, "Dīwān ᶜĀ'ishah al-Bāᶜūnīyah," 113-15, and al-ᶜAlāwī, *ᶜĀ'ishah al-Bāᶜūnīyah*, 44-47, and 185-212, for an edited Arabic edition of the poem.

26. ᶜĀ'ishah al-Bāᶜūnīyah, *Dīwān ᶜĀ'ishah al-Bāᶜūnīyah* (= *Fayḍ al-Faḍl*), Cairo: Dār al-Kutub al-Miṣrīyah, microfilm 29322 of MS 431 (Shiᶜr Taymūr), and and *Dīwān Fayḍ al-Faḍl wa-Jam ᶜ al-*Shaml, edited by Mahdi As'ad ᶜArrar (Beirut, 2010).

27. Ibid., 4/71.

28. Ibid., 5/71.

29. Ibid., 218-19/326.

as the volume proceeds, the name of ᶜĀ'ishah's second Sufi guide, Yaḥyā al-'Urmawī, begins to appear, strongly suggesting that ᶜĀ'ishah composed these poems after al-Ḥawwārī's death in 900/1495.[30] ᶜĀ'ishah seems to have regarded the *Emanation of Grace* as a work in progress, and this may explain why none of the manuscripts cite a completion date for the original work. Further, ᶜĀ'ishah refers by title to her other writings in several places in the *Emanation of Grace*, yet she does not mention any of the odes that she composed while in Egypt, and so the *Emanation of Grace* may have ended when ᶜĀ'ishah left Damascus for Egypt in 919/1513.[31]

Another distinguishing feature of the *Emanation of Grace* is that ᶜĀ'ishah often added a short note at the beginning of many poems. Nearly every poem is preceded by the phrase: "From God's inspiration upon her" (*wa-min fatḥi Allāhi ᶜalayhā*), or, more often, "From His inspiration upon her" (*wa-min fatḥihi ᶜalayhā*). In many instances, this is followed by a few additional words regarding the poem. Not surprisingly, in the first quarter of the *Emanation of Grace*, we find poems prefaced as having been composed "in the early days" (*fī ayyām al-bidāyah*).[32] In other cases throughout the volume, ᶜĀ'ishah notes a poem's topic, such as praise of the Prophet, or the importance of recollection (*dhikr*).[33] Yet still more extraordinary are ᶜĀ'ishah's references to her mystical or emotional state when she composed specific poems as when "rapture was intense" (*wa-jadda wajdun*) or "from His inspiration upon her during a session of mystical *audition*" (*wa-min fatḥihi ᶜalayhā fī ḥaḍrati-s-samāᶜi*).[34] To have such information for poems is rare in any literary tradition, and so we are extremely fortunate that ᶜĀ'ishah cared to share aspects of her mystical life with her readers in what may be her spiritual diary.

This candor is in keeping with ᶜĀ'ishah's view of herself as an accomplished mystic and spiritual guide. Many of her poems are *munājāt*, secret prayers or intimate monologues with God, and they usually consist of two or three verses. In one such poem from "the early days," ᶜĀ'ishah says:[35]

> Whenever the fates make your servant recall
> someone besides you, by God, it does no good.
> For memory of you is hidden deep in the heart,
> and You know what I reveal and conceal.

---

30. Ibid., 314/435.

31. Ibid., 218-20/326-27; 296-97/414.

32. E.g., ibid., 5/72; 18/92, 22/98; 36/117.

33. E.g., ibid, 19/88; 29/107; 31/110; 115/211; 208/314.

34. E.g., ibid., 5-7/73-76; 10/80; 15/87; 33/114; 38-39/120-21; 76/167; 79/170; 83/175; 99/193; 105/199; 137/235; 212/319.

35. Ibid., 5/72.

The poems in the *Emanation of Grace* take up a number of religious and mystical themes, especially the love of God and His Prophet, the importance of recollection, spiritual *intoxication*, and mystical union. In nearly every poem, ᶜĀ'ishah employs key terms from the Sufi lexicon to underscore her mystical allusions, and very often she calls upon God using one of His ninty-nine "Beautiful Names" (e.g. *al-ᶜAlīm*: "the Omniscient; *al-Wadūd*: "the Beloved").[36] Most of these poems are devotional in tone, with clear diction and style, though ᶜĀ'ishah often adds a rhetorical flourish, popular in verse at that time. Moreover, in these poems, ᶜĀ'ishah explored the full range of Arabic rhymes, meters, and poetic forms, including the quatrain (*dū bayt*), the ode (*qaṣīdah*), the love poem (*ghazal*), poems in praise of Muhammad (*al-madīḥ al-nabawī*), as well as verse in praise of wine (*khamrīyah*). Wine was a major theme in pre-Islamic verse, and even after the coming of Islam, wine remained a popular subject in classical Arabic poetry. Though the Qur'ān forbids the consumption of wine by Muslims on earth, it goes on to declare that the residents of Paradise will "be served a choice wine sealed with musk" (83:25-27). Some Muslim poets, including Abū Nuwās (d.c. 200/815), certainly praised the earthly wine of the grape, while Sufi writers, including the Egyptian poet ᶜUmar Ibn al-Fāriḍ (d. 632/1235) and ᶜĀ'ishah al-Bāᶜūnīyah, invoked wine as a metaphor for God's intoxicating love and the future bliss of Paradise.[37]

ᶜĀ'ishah also composed in newer poetic forms, and in several poems, she included and elaborated on an earlier poem by another author (*takhmīs*). In one such instance, ᶜĀ'ishah expanded on an ode ascribed to the founder of her order, ᶜAbd al-Qādir al-Jīlānī, to exalt his high saintly status.[38] In several instances, her poems have multiple internal rhymes using a form that was popular for sermons (*kān wa-kān*), and appropriately, in these poems, ᶜĀ'ishah gives religious advice to Sufi novices and adepts alike.[39] In addition, ᶜĀ'ishah sometimes composed in more popular and colloquial forms of her day, including strophic poems using the *musammaṭ*, *zajal,* and *muwashshaḥ* forms. Her *muwashshaḥ*, in particular, often have refrains, and they may have been chanted or sung in sessions of mystical *audition*,

---

36. See "*Al-Asmā' al-Ḥusnā*," (L. Gardet), in *Encyclopaedia of Islam*, 2nd ed., ed. H.A.R. Gibb, et. al. (Leiden, 1960), 1:714-17.

37. See Philip F. Kennedy, *Abu Nuwas: A Genius of Poetry* (Oxford, 2005), and Th. Emil Homerin, *The Wine of Love and Life: Ibn Fāriḍ's al-Khamrīah and al-Qayṣarī's Quest for Meaning* (Chicago, 2005).

38. For *takhmīs*, see "allusion and intertextuality," (W.P. Heinrichs), in *Encyclopedia of Arabic Literature*, 1:82-83, and Rabābiᶜah, *ᶜĀ'ishah al-Bāᶜūnīyah: Shāᶜirah*, 123-38. The translation of this poem will be found in the anthology.

39. See "*kān wa-kān*," (W. Stoetzer) in *Encyclopedia of Arabic Literature*, 2:425-426, and the examples in the anthology.

known as *samāᶜ*.[40] ᶜĀ'ishah tells us at the beginning of several poems that she attended such sessions, where Sufi masters and their disciples gather to recollect God, chant the Qur'ān, and praise His prophet Muhammad. This is often followed by chanters or singers who recite mystical verse, as the audience might sway in unison to induce a trance and a mystical experience. Often, participants join in the chant, especially of God's names, and in one *muwashshaḥ*, ᶜĀ'ishah included such a refrain after every strophe: *Yā Hū, yā Hū, yā Allāh* ("O, Him, O, Him, O, God!").[41]

As the *Emanation of Grace* continues, we encounter more strophic and longer poems, and, in many of them, a confident ᶜĀ'ishah assumes the role of the knowledgeable mystical guide who instructs the Sufi novice. This is clearly the case in one of her longest poems in the collection, composed of 252 verses on a variety of mystical themes. This poem could be entitled the *al-Tā'īyah al-Bāᶜūnīyah* ("Bāᶜūnī's Ode in T"), since she modeled this poem on Ibn al-Fāriḍ's Sufi classic the *Naẓm al-Sulūk* ("Poem of the Sufi Way"), commonly known as the *al-Tā'īyah al-Kubrā* ("Ode in T – Major").[42] Both poems rhyme in the letter "t" and begin in praise of the wine of love that leads to spiritual intoxication and an eventual union with the divine *Beloved* during the Hajj pilgrimage. ᶜĀ'ishah also follows Ibn al-Fāriḍ when she invokes the "ancient *covenant*" as the original source of her love for God. In Sufi circles, this refers to the "Day of the Covenant" (*yawm al-mīthāq*) alluded to in the Qur'ān:

> And when your Lord drew from the loins of the children of Adam their progeny and made them bear witness against themselves: "Am I not your Lord?" They said: "Indeed, yes! We so witness . . . (7:172)
>
> Recall (*adhkurū*) the blessings upon you from your Lord and His covenant (*mīthāq*) that He confirmed with you when you said: "We hear and obey!" (5:7)

ᶜĀ'ishah, Ibn al-Fāriḍ, and many other Sufis believed that God called forth humanity to take this covenant in pre-eternity thus bringing about the original loving encounter between the divine *spirit* (*rūḥ*) within each human

40. See "*muwashshaḥ*," (L. Alvarez) and "strophic poetry," (W. Stoetzer) in *Encyclopedia of Arabic Literature*, 2:563-66; 2:737, and the examples in the anthology. For a useful introduction to ᶜĀ'ishah's poetics, with brief examples drawn largely from the *Fayḍ al-Faḍl*, see Rabābiᶜah, *ᶜĀ'ishah al-Bāᶜūnīyah: Shāᶜirah*, 68-400.

41. The entire poem is translated below. For an account of a *samāᶜ* session, see Th. Emil Homerin, *From Arab Poet to Muslim Saint* (Cairo, 2001), 78-83, and also see Meir, "Dervish Dance," and Jean During, *Musique et extase* (Paris, 1988).

42. ᶜĀ'ishah al-Bāᶜūnīyah, *Fayḍ al-Faḍl*, 139-51/237-51, and Th. Emil Homerin, *ᶜUmar Ibn al-Fāriḍ: Sufi Verse, Saintly Life* (New York, 2001), 67-291.

being, and God. It is the recollection (*dhikr*) of this moment that may lead to the *annihilation* (*fanā'*) of the selfish soul and the spirit's return to *abide* (*baqā'*) in God's oneness (*tawḥīd*), as ᶜĀ'ishah declares in her *Emanations of Grace*:[43]

He who tastes the love of God vanishes
from his selfish soul and cares, to abide in Him,

Annihilated without an eye or trace remaining,
rapt in beholding the awesome beauty of His love.

All of his fanciful desires pass away
in preference for what comes from his beloved.

He regards His prohibition as the greatest gift,
and so, too, banishment from being near Him.

Vision of Him leads the lover to melt away
as the epiphany refines him.

With such a mystical vision, creation can be grasped for what it truly is: manifestations of God's Beautiful Names and Attributes originated and ordered through the primordial Light of Muhammad. According to one tradition Muhammad said: "I was a prophet when Adam was still between water and clay," and his Prophetic Light was believed to be God's first emanation and the instrument of all subsequent creation. Thus, while the Light of Muhammad shines in pre-eternity, it illuminates creation as well. All of the prophets and the saints, too, have partaken of this Light, though it shone most brightly in the prophet Muhammad, who the Qur'ān (33:46) calls "a shining lamp" (*sirāj munīr*).[44] This Light appears in ᶜĀ'ishah's *Ode in T* and other poems, as she calls the spiritual seeker to love the Prophet selflessly and to recollect God with humility so that by an emanation of God's grace, the lover may taste and see that all the world glows with God's supernal light, as the Qur'ān declares (24:35):

> God is the light of the heavens and the earth. The semblance of His light is like a niche in which is a lamp, the lamp in a glass. The glass is like a shining star lit from a blessed tree, an olive, of neither east nor west, whose oil would seem to shine even if not touched by fire. Light upon light, God guides to His light whom He wills, and God strikes parables for humanity, for God knows everything!

---

43. ᶜĀ'ishah al-Bāᶜūnīyah, *Fayḍ al-Faḍl*, 43/125.

44. See Annemarie Schimmel, *And Muhammad Is His Messenger* (Chapel Hill, NC, 1985), 123-43.

On Translation

Given the large size and many poems of ᶜĀ'ishah al-Bāᶜūnīyah's *Emanation of Grace and the Gathering Union*, I have chosen to edit and translate a selection of her poetry representative of her mystical themes and poetic style. Since the *Emanation of Grace* appears to be arranged chronologically, I have left the poems in their original order, with one exception, the *al-Tā'īyah al-Bāᶜūnīyah* or *ᶜĀ'ishah al-Bāᶜūnīyah's Ode in T*. This is a very long poem with many allusions to the Qur'ān, Sufism, and verse by Ibn al-Fāriḍ, and so I have placed this poem last accompanied by a brief commentary and analysis of the poem.

ᶜĀ'ishah's poems have been lovingly read and copied for centuries, and so they deserve a reasonable poetic counterpart in English. When translating her verse, I have been concerned not only with form and content, but also with a poem's tones, moods, and deeper meanings. Toward this end, my own method of translation generally follows that laid out by Robert Bly in *The Eight Stages of Translation*.[45] The first stage is to pick a poem and provide a rather literal, if awkward, translation. Here is one of ᶜĀ'ishah's couplets:[46]

tawājadtu ḥattā lāḥa lī fī tawājudī
wujūdan ᶜani-l-aghyāri lil-qalbi ṣārifu
fa-lā wājidun illā li-ḥālī wājidu
fa-lā ᶜārifun illā bi-mā qultu ᶜārifu

I sought/was affected by passion, until he/it appeared
as/with/in my passionate condition
an existence for the heart distracted from others
(or: pure of different things).
And there is no one who is excited [by love]
except he is finding my state,
and there is no expert/connoisseur except he is knowing
what I say.

The second stage of translation is to probe the meaning of the poem in context of the poet and her/his literary and cultural traditions. We are fortunate to know quite a bit about ᶜĀ'ishah's life and verse, particularly that she was a Sufi who composed mystical poetry. Indeed, a number of words in this couplet are common Sufi technical terms, many associated with the mystical meditation and chanting practice known as audition (*samāᶜ*): *tawājad* ("to seek or experience mystical rapture"), *wujūd* ("existence," "being," "finding" [God or ecstasy]), *qalb* ("heart," "site of inspiration"), *aghyār*

45. Robert Bly, *The Eight Stages of Translation* (Boston, 1983), 13-49.
46. ᶜĀ'ishah al-Bāᶜūnīyah, *Fayḍ al-Faḍl*), 6/74.

("others," "things other" than God, "difference and change"), *wājid* ("one overcome by rapture," "one who finds"), *ᶜārif* ("one who knows," "gnostic"), and *ḥāl* (a mystical "state").[47] So in the third stage, adjustments are made to bring these elements into the English translation:

I was in rapture, until he appeared to me in my rapture
    with an existence for the heart pure of others.
And there is no one who is in rapture except he finds my state,
    and there is no gnostic except he knows what I say.

The fourth and fifth stages aim to smooth the translation into more natural English, paying particular attention to the original's tone and mood. In the first verse, ᶜĀ'ishah attests to having found God and/or ecstasy. This, in turn leads to her claim, in the second verse, to speak authoritatively about union. Further, the parallel construction used in the last verse: "there is no . . . but," implies that she is now a qualified Sufi master:

I was rapt, until he appeared to me in my rapture
    with an existence for the heart pure of others.
For there is no one in rapture but he finds my state,
    and there is no gnostic but he knows what I say.

Stages six and seven focus on the sounds and rhythms of both the original and the translation. The Arabic meter of the couplet is *ṭawīl*, literally, "long," and this meter together with the many long vowels in both verses, suggest that the tone of the couplet is rather measured, not sharp or manic. Moreover, in the original, ᶜĀ'ishah plays on the Arabic root *w-j-d* (i.e., *tawājadtu, tawājudī, wujūdan, wājidun, wājidu*) with its allusions to being, discovery, and ecstasy, albeit with various nuances. Further, the repetition of the root *w-j-d* creates assonance and alliteration in the couplet, which are difficult to duplicate in translation. Nevertheless, other sound patterns may present themselves during the fine-tuning of stage eight.

In my final version, I chose to play on the English "rapture" with "rapt" and "ravished," while changing "but" to "save" in order to establish a faint alliteration with "state" and "say." Similarly, I decided on "free from" for "pure of" for an alliteration, which resonates with "finds" in verse two. As for *wujūd*, this word can mean "existence," or "being," yet in terms of the heart's mystical state, "finding" ecstasy is probably intended, though this sounds awkward, so I opted for "ecstasy" alone. Finally, in the last verse, I tried to apply assonance ("So no," "no gnostic . . . knows") along with a homonym ("no," "know") to approximate ᶜĀ'ishah's parallelism and her

47. E.g., see *Al-Qushayri's Epistle on Sufism*, trans. by Alexander D. Knysh (Reading, UK, 2007), 83-87, and William C. Chittick, *The Sufi Path of Knowledge* (Albany, 1989), 3-4, 10, 106-109, 212-13, 223.

scheme of repeating the same word, but with different meanings (*wājid*: "one ravished," "finding;" *ᶜārif*: "gnostic," "knowing") as required by the rules of Arabic poetry:

I was rapt, until in my rapture, he appeared
in an existence for the heart free from others.
So no one is ravished save he finds my state,
and there is no gnostic save he knows what I say.

Still, as usually happens in any translation between languages, several problems persist when translating Arabic to English. First, as in the above couplet, ᶜĀ'ishah often uses terms that have a specific meaning within Islamic mysticism, and so, I have tried to be consistent in my translation of these terms, many of which will be found in the glossary at the end of this book. Second, in Arabic, most words are either feminine or masculine in gender. While this usually does not pose a problem for the more gender neutral English, it is essential, at times, to bring over the gender of a word. Finally, Arabic does not have capitalization, which can be an important marker in English, particularly when speaking about Him, i.e., God. Both matters are relevant when dealing with the lover and beloved of many of ᶜĀ'ishah's poems. Though her beloved is often God, in some poems, her lover may also be the prophet Muhammad, her Sufi masters, and, perhaps, her husband, too. Therefore, I have not capitalized any nouns or pronouns referring to the beloved unless ᶜĀ'ishah indicates the beloved's divine identity, either by naming Him with one of His ninety-nine Beautiful Names, or with some other clear reference. An example of these dilemmas is well illustrated in the opening verses to one of her last poems in the *Emanation of Grace*:[48]

These are the gardens of eternity,
fulfilling what was promised.
They were opened wide,
and the Beloved's beauty appeared there.
He said: "O woman whose existence
was consumed in Mine,
"I have preserved you in Me forever
as My generous gift.
"So you are living in Me,
summoned to witness Me."

In the second verse of this poem, the word for Beloved is *al-wadūd*, one of God's Beautiful names, so I have capitalized this word and all subse-

48. ᶜĀ'ishah al-Bāᶜūnīyah, *Fayḍ al-Faḍl*), 310/430. The entire poem is translated below.

quent pronouns to Him. The Arabic of v. 3 reads: *wa-qāla: yā man tafānā wujūduhā fī wujūdī.* Here, ᶜĀ'ishah is using the technical language of the Sufis regarding the annihilation or passing away (*fanā'*) of the mystic in God so as to abide (*baqā'*) in love (v. 4). The third verse, then, may be translated roughly as: "He said: O one whose existence has passed away in My existence." The Arabic term *man*, "one who" can be read as masculine or feminine, singular or plural depending on what follows, and it is the feminine pronominal suffix (*hā*) attached to the first occurrence of "existence" (*wujūdu*) that informs us that God is speaking to a woman, hence my translation "O woman whose existence . . . " But, then in v. 5, ᶜĀ'ishah makes a pun impossible to bring over in translation, so I mention it here. God says: "So you are living in Me;" the word for "living" is *ᶜā'ishah.*

Emanations of Grace

Mystical Poems by
ᶜĀ'ishah al-Bāᶜūnīyah
(d. 923/1517)

In the name of God, the Compassionate, the Merciful

God inspired ᶜĀ'ishah, who lives with Him after He annihilated her in Him, one blessed with the love of Him and the love of His people. She is related by birth to Yūsuf ibn Aḥmad al-Bāᶜūnī, and in spirit to the unique axis and the beauty of religion, Ismāᶜīl al-Ḥawwārī.

Praise be to God, who confers His help upon whomever He wishes, who attracts to Him completely those whom He chooses by His hand, with a praise that bears grace and grants union. I bear witness that there is no deity but God alone, who has no partner and nothing like Him, no match nor equal. This is a testimony appropriate to His unicity, as He desires, and one mentioning, to His satisfaction, His glorification. This is a testimony that annihilates "I" in "He," and brings union nigh by means of the divine attractions. I bear witness that the most perfect chosen one, the most blessed apostle, the one revealing the merciful secret, the lamp of the lordly light, the ocean of eternal emanation, peerless in clear contemplation, is His trustworthy Muhammad, His unshakeable apostle, may God bless him with prayers that will fulfill his wish and grant him his hope. May God bless those who possess revelation among the prophets and those who posses determination among the apostles, and the Prophet's family, companions, and those who followed them, and the people of all the other pious ones. May God bless them as long as a sad person yearns so that a beloved will be generous, and may He give them the greatest peace and exalt them!

May God, most high, sanctify the heart of the exalted, awesome and brilliant axis, the peerless, universal, and lovely savior, one speaking with the God's command: "My foot is on the neck of every saint of God!", the lordly axis, the eternally realized one, Muḥyī Dīn ᶜAbd al-Qādir al-Jīlānī, may his heart be sanctified commiserate to his high station, and may his wish and hope be fulfilled, for truly, He is generous and noble, gracious and merciful!

May God, most high, sanctify the heart of him whom I have served thereby bringing me providence, whose glance upon me brought blessings, and whose concern for me honored me. For it graciously came to pass during the Primordial Covenant that my succor would come from him, and I would learn from him, and that he would be my annihilation and abiding, my honesty and good faith, my intoxication and sobriety, my stability and effacement, and that he would polish my heart, remove my veil, and bring about my cure. He would also be my pull and attraction for my drawing near, and he would always be my refreshment and my happiness, and my means to ascend to the apex of my union to attain my desire, and to realize, from him and his succor, my hope. He is the master, the authoritative and exalted leader, the peerless universal axis and support, the axis of the eminent men of the time, crown of the great ones of the age, the master, the imam, the one with total authority over the elite and the common, the caliph on behalf of the best of humanity, my master and exemplar, my leader and my support, the lordly axis eternally favored, the lamp of the light of the chosen Prophet, Jamāl al-Dīn Ismāʿīl al-Ḥawwārī; may he attain his wish and realize his prosperity, for truly, God is generous and noble, gracious and merciful. May God sanctify the spirits of the saints and those brought near, and all the rest of the righteous ones, with His blessing and generosity. Amen!

Now, this is a book whose mystical meanings are choice, and its being written down is a divine blessing. Good fortune has named it *The Emanation of Grace and the Gathering of Union*. It contains poetry inspired by Him regarding intimate conversations with the divine and spiritual meanings, states of grace and mystical struggle, matters of desire and passionate ways, serving as a distraction to one who was consumed by desire and drawn by the collar by yearning, who was treated roughly by the beloved, and made ill by the physician, so that talk and gossip swirled about him. Then, he attained union, and separation was no more, and God, the exalted, made him the means to union with abundant shares of the epiphanies of glory and beauty, receiving him with approval and good fortune, benefits and favors, and He made him acceptable to [the prophet Muhammad], who is especially close [to God], and to all of the axes and the rest of the beloveds. And He is generous, giving beyond measure! (2-5/69-72).

A secret prayer (pg. 5/72):

O my strength, my king, my greatest goal,
    my fickle heart prays toward you!
Lord, I beseech You with all
    a worshipper can do when he calls You.
Kindly keep me from harm, make my dream come true,
    and let my heart have its wildest wish and desire!

From God's inspiration upon her and that was in the early days (5/72):

Whenever the fates make your servant recall
    someone besides you, by God, it does no good.
For memory of you is hidden deep in the heart,
    and You know what I reveal and conceal.

Also from His inspiration (5/72):

I am content with what God wants for me;
    I commit my whole life to Him.
I turn to Him, seek refuge in Him, cling to Him,
    for I can rely on no one save Him!

Also from His inspiration (5/72):

The burden of my provisions grew completely light
    when I trusted in what the Provider guaranteed.
Human kind and all they gather and collect will pass away
    while the everlasting is God, His stores imperishable!

Also from His inspiration (5/73):

Drop all your plans
    and give it all to God.
Entrust the matter to Him
    whose hands hold all power!

Also from His inspiration, and rapture was intense (5-6/73-74):

1. With noble invocation of the One, Creator,
   refresh a heart melted by longing.

2. Singer, lift up His praise and repeat it;
   Sāqī, pass round His ancient wine of love.

3. For life has passed in desire to drink it,
   though I never won a taste, no, not a taste.

4. See how it revived impassioned souls
   brought to ruin and destruction.

5. See how it made them disappear
   from all the world since they fell for it.

6. See how it drove them love-mad and crazy,
   shattered by rapture and craving,

7. See how it melted hearts now flowing down
   in tears from large round eyes.

8. See how it brought a dead love back to life.
   O, how many strong lovers have died!

9. It is a wine ever appearing
   to man as the rising sun,

10. And when its bouquet spreads forth,
    it covers all the world and existence.

11. When will I win its quenching taste
    passing me away in that abiding beauty?[1]

---

1. In the final verse of this poem, ᶜĀ'ishah plays on Sufi terms for mystical union, *fanā'* ("*annihilation*," "*passing away*") and *baqā* ("*abiding*"), in context of the Qur'ānic declaration (55:26-27): "All things on earth are passing away (*fānin*), while the majestic and beneficent countenance of your Lord abides (*yabqā*)."

Also from His inspiration (6/74):

> It is glory enough for the lovers if their True Lord
> is their beloved, alone, without creation,
> and it is honor enough if they seek and aspire
> for nothing but His satisfaction.

And from His inspiration upon her concerning required mystical stages (6/74):

> I was rapt, until in my rapture he appeared
> in an existence for the heart free from others.
> So no one is ravished save he finds my state,
> and there is no gnostic save he knows what I say.

And from His inspiration upon her (6/74):

> Praise be to you, my Lord, for the amazing grace
> You bestowed on me, You generous one!
> Now every member of my body has a tongue
> reciting thanks to You, my Lord and greatest patron!

And from His inspiration upon her as a mystical state appeared (6/75):

> Since my heart is strong and vigilant,
> and all of me recalls Him within and without,
> I will pay no heed to all who blame me
> though they gather an army for war.

And similarly from His inspiration upon her (6/75):

> It is naught save a deluge that will appear,
> as the clouds covering the heart float away.
> Then the sun of truth will reveal to us a vista
> and conceal us from us as we abide with Him there.

And from [His inspiration], a secret prayer (6/75):

> My God, my Lord, my greatest goal,
> I beseech you, in the name of the beloved guide, Muhammad,
> for Your favor to draw me near Your presence
> where the lovers reach the most glorious source!

Emanations of Grace

From His inspiration upon her, and patience was gone as loving desire increased (7-8/76-77):

1. What can I do since my heart fell in love?
   I care for nothing else.

2. The critics went on and on in their blame,
   and they protested and told me to forget him.

3. Blaming me, they had no pity for my state; no,
   they weren't looking after me or my fate.

4. Rebuking me, they warned of different things;
   had been fair and described themselves, what a warning!

5. Though they hurt with their blame, they did well,
   since they mentioned him often in their talk.

6. But they're just excuses; they have never tasted passion!
   They will never move on with their sorry baggage.

7. For the hallow man is not like one anxious and troubled;
   those fast asleep are not wide-eyed with desire.

8. The lover has no recourse save the flow of tears and grief
   when he falls ill after the beloveds depart.

9. My condition reveals the one I secretly love,
   yet secrecy is prescribed for true lovers!

10. I kept him secret for a time till love overcame me,
    and the guarded hidden secret came out.

11. So I feigned madness as my state,
    though, by God, madness never touched me.

12. My heart has the spring of life in death in him,
    and my exaltation arose as I bent low before him.

13. He is the lover for whom no equal can be found,
    nor will a brave knight ever equal the likes of him.

14. By him, I made the ancient covenant to Him,
    so my pledge was firm and will never waver!

Emanations of Grace

From His inspiration upon her during a transcendental state (*ḥālah mughayyibah*) (10-11/80-81):

1. Who forgives the sinful woman, save Your pardon?
   Who remembers the wretch, save Your grace?

2. Who aids the poor woman, save Your generous gift?
   Who mends the broken, save Your favor?

3. Where is refuge for the outcast, save Your door?
   Who protects the fugitive, save Your glory?

4. What strengthens the weak woman, save Your aid?
   What helps the afflicted, save Your kindness?

5. When my sins grow in number,
   who will forgive me other than You, Lord of lords?

6. You are the *Real*, all else is vain,
   and everything manifests Your divine names:

7. Giver of Life, Taker of life, the First,
   the Last, the Hidden, the Manifest,

8. Powers of the awesome Sultan in which
   minds are effaced and vision overwhelmed.

9. Lord, divine Lord, my master, my *savior*, my helper,
   all is in awe of You.

10. My selfish soul and its actions,
    all of my states and limited reason

11. Are lapses and misdeeds and shameful sins.
    By Your great glory, please forgive them!

12. Things arose in me You know too well;
    my Lord and Savior, protect me!

13. With Your grace, look upon all my affairs
    with a glance turning ruin to riches,

14. And render my business worthy of Your great gift
    turning my weakness to strength.

15. Choose for me blessings that will help my heart
    turn to see and behold You,

16. And favor me with Your servant, the axis,
    to whom the great ones bow with deference.

17. Continue to aid me with his gifts
    so that my heart will soar in his sky.

18. So favor me with Your servant, the axis,
    successor to the splendid, praiseworthy Prophet,

19. My guide, Jamāl al-Dīn Ismāʿīl:
    may he continue to witness and be present

20. Alone, abiding in the splendor of Your essence!
    My Lord, make abundant my share from You,

21. Fulfill my hope, answer my prayer,
    and guide a bewildered heart.

22. My Lord, bless the Prophet with peace
    and honor, glory and reverence,

23. And his family and close companions
    and those who follow with worthy deeds!

Emanations of Grace

From His inspiration upon her as was needed [to refute her critics] (15-16/87-88):

1. I went out to the garden
   to refresh my sight
   with God's perfect handiwork
   enclosed there.

2. Yet they blamed me and said:
   "You claim love and passion,
   but clearly you busy your heart
   with other things!"

3. So I replied:
   "My Lord God forbid!
   I only went for admonition,
   not temptation,

4. "For from my strong desire
   for the designer, our Lord,
   I looked to the traces
   where love hides.

5. "I only want to see
   their reflection of His designs,
   my heart at peace
   in contemplation.

6. "And why not?
   For the signs of Him in His creation
   are there for those
   who wish to clearly see.

7. "Indeed, the Beloved
   does not lead
   the one who loves Him
   by any sweeter sign.

8. "These are nothing
   but sights of His power
   whose sense was meant
   for my eyes."

And from His inspiration upon her during a mystical *audition* (*samā*[c]) (15-16/88-89):

1. My friend, say again
   the name of one I love.

2. Despite my devotion to come to him,
   I can't get enough as long as I live!

3. Tales of passion for him
   have been told by me,

4. And in spreading them arose
   a new life that will never end.

5. So I can't forget him;
   I can't wait or be without him;

6. I can't be away from him.
   No. I can't cope.

7. My tears flow from passion;
   my heart is grilled by love

8. For between my ribs is a fire
   burning me within.

9. Critics blame my heart,
   but, my friends, it won't be turned

10. By their honeyed lies
    for they are masters of deceit.

11. For when I complained of my state,
    my love sickness, and tribulation,

12. My heart answered:
    "This is not the way of one who loves.

13. "One stripped bare before love
    casts off complaining.

14. "To die for him is nothing;
    misfortunes are adored for him!"

15. Do you think I can win
    his nearness curing all my ills?

16. Being close to him is my highest goal
    and furthest desire,

17. And I don't mean by this, old loves
    like Salmā or ᶜAlmā or Hind.

18. My only aim is him
    who knows the heart and love talk,

19. One everlasting God
    Who shaped all creation.

20. From Him, I hope for an honored place
    in the safe Abode of Eternity.[2]

---

2. In verse 17 of this poem, ᶜĀ'ishah states that her lover is not "Salmā, ᶜAlmā, or Hind." These are the names of several beloveds of Arab legend, and ᶜĀ'ishah dismisses them to underscore the divine nature of her love. As ᶜĀ'ishah undoubtedly knew, the celebrated Arab poet Abū Nuwās (d.c. 200/815) had earlier cast aside the loves of legend in his preference for wine; see Abū Nuwās, *Dīwān*, ed. Ewald Wagner (Wiesbaden, 1988), 3:106, and Philip F. Kennedy, *Abu Nuwas: A Genius of Poetry* (Oxford, 2005). In verse 19, ᶜĀ'ishah paraphrases the first two verses of Qur'ān 112: "Say He is God, the one, God the everlasting."

From His inspiration upon her, and that was in the early days (26-27/105-106):

1. Praise of God's prophet quickens the soul,
   it drives away doubt, worries, and grief,

2. Spirits find rest, eyes cry in delight,
   and bodies dance, there's no holding back.

3. Ears savor the sound, the heart throbs in the ribs,
   and lips speak, though they were dumb.

4. Lovers are moved, and longing is easy,
   one bewildered by passion is struck down as if mad,

5. And favors are hoped for, and desires are sought,
   while cares fly away along with despair.

6. No wonder, for he is the chosen of all His worshippers
   and the foundation of faith:

7. Muhammad, sent with mercy to humanity
   though they be of different races.

8. He has miracles beyond measure or count
   whose nature awes humans and *jinn*.

9. A prophet who led us to guidance with the holy Qur'ān,
   removing the filth of sin.

10. From his hands, fresh water flowed refreshing to all,
    and a tree sprang to life though it had been dead.

11. Silent stones in his hand shouted his praise,
    and from their good fortune a seedling bore fruit.

12. For him, the full, bright moon was split asunder;
    for him, the sun was veiled, as the Throne Lord willed.

13. Master of the two worlds, the best of humanity,
    the one for whom God ended our ignorance,

14. Help me! Help me, my master, with intercession
    on a day when the newborns' hair turns gray.

15. No intercessor's word will be heard save yours,
    you, the *best of creation* among humans and jinn.

16. Be my advocate when Hell appears
    so that its flame will not touch my body.

17. Watch over me all life long, and at my death,
    when the grave embraces me,

18. When my breath subsides, and my lamp goes out,
    and all my sense and senses vanish.

19. You are my hope then, and now,
    for I will never see anxiety amid your kindness.

20. So bless me with your light to clear my vision,
    and cure a heart struck by misfortune.

21. May God's prayers and peace be upon you
    as long as the soul longs to see you,

22. As long as the dove coos in the trees,
    and darts among the gardens' tangled branches,

23. And as long as the shining sun appears at morn,
    tingeing the sky with deepening hues.[3]

---

3. In verses 8-12 of this poem, ᶜĀ'ishah alludes to several miracles ascribed to Muhammad. For a recounting of these and other tales, see Annemarie Schimmel, *And Muhammad is His Messenger* (Chapel Hill, NC, 1985), 67-80.

From His inspiration upon her as she stood before the Noble Stone, may the greatest prayers and peace be upon its site [in the Kaᶜbah in Mecca] (29/107-108):

1. I have come to tell my story to my intercessor
   with all my humility, remorse, and submission,

2. And I tell you, who are the best of humanity,
   that I have squandered away life's treasure.

3. I have carried my load, I have earned my sins
   that draw out my groans of suffering.

4. My misdeeds have multiplied, so many from me,
   and how long have I cried.

5. Now, I have shown up at your door, my master,
   that you might be my intercessor before God.

6. I have come repenting of awful acts that I have done,
   yes, and of my evil ways.

7. So intercede with forgiveness for what I have done,
   and with acceptance of my return and repentance.

8. Look upon me with a glance that will place me
   with the righteous in an exalted station.

9. God's prayers and peace be upon you, *Banner of Guidance*,
   as long as fragrance spreads from flowers in spring,

10. As long as one yearning is pleased by your presence
    where my longing and confession are sweet.

From His inspiration upon her regarding her certainty of the nobility of recollection (*dhikr*) (31/110):

> When sin soils the hearts,
>   and their light grows dim and dark,
> Then recollection of God is their polish
>   wiping the spots away.
> In recollection of God, how many hearts
>   remove the rust, revealing the light within.

From His inspiration upon her, a secret prayer (34/114):

> In recalling You, my Lord, the spirit finds rest,
>   and the soul is relieved of worry and stress.
> One who strives in his world to remember You,
>   attains glad tidings and happiness.

From His inspiration upon her as spiritual guidance (34/115):

> Three things can save one who would be saved:
>   sincerity, belief in God, and hope.
> How many sinners in a jam
>   have found a way out with them!

And from His inspiration upon her (34/115):

> Cheers to those busy with their Lord,
>   engaged with God alone.
> This leads to success and happiness
>   as they walk in God's light on the shining path.

And from His inspiration upon her (34/115):

> I could do nothing about my existence,
>   looking after my selfish soul
>   and giving it what it fancied.
> There is no refuge
>   save clinging to a master
>   whose grace tames and trains the soul.

From His inspiration upon her, for spiritual guidance and realization (34-36/115-117):

1. Leave society,
   leave it all;
   seek the Lord,
   and union will come.

2. Stand at the door,
   kiss the floor,
   obey the rules,
   and hear: “Welcome!”

3. Give up sleep,
   keep with the fast,
   follow the mystics,
   and separation will cease.

4. Make the effort,
   resigned to God,
   attain the goal,
   and receive His grace.

5. You, serving up wine,
   the cups’ secret within
   revives the spirits
   and amazes the mind.

6. Grant me a gift,
   give the wine straight,
   perhaps, then I’ll be quenched
   and find union.

7. For the love within me
   has worn me out,
   and so effaced
   all of me,

8. As passion rose up,
   and love
   nearly scorched my heart,
   leading to madness.

9. Yes, the desires
brought this down—
and my heart
could not bear it—

10. To pull back the veil
and give me a drink
of the wine of love,
sweetest of sweets.

11. Since the leader was kind,
I said: "You, with the cup,
do you see there
a portion for me?"

12. How many this cup
has robbed of sensation,
how many people
have died.

13. They witnessed a sign:
His most brilliant light,
and minds saw
a source unseen.

14. My blamer, enough,
could you but see
His glowing light
when it appears,

15. Then you would forgive
and defend for me
any effaced
when they are blamed.

16. I will never forget
His glorious light
adorning Him
when I bowed in submission.

17. O, great lovers,
our time was pure,
and longing was quenched,
so praise the Lord.

18. My Master has blessed us,
contented with us,
so He received us
with: "Welcome!"

19. The veils were thrown back
with the waning of pride,
and He granted nearness
as a grace to me,

20. Since my heart was drawn,
my friends,
to exalted *nearness*
that it did not deserve.

21. For the heart doesn't earn
the states it receives;
they are the gift
of the Lord's beneficence.

22. Yes, pure grace,
from a just God,
Who bestows favor
on those He prefers.

23. Giver of grace,
Master, help me,
annihilate me,
in You, Lord.

24. Leave not a shadow
of something behind,
that I might live
and grasp union.

25. My Lord, guide me
to what brings me near You,
and annihilate me
in Your radiant face,

26. And from the *chosen one*,
spread the lights
to my bewildered heart
and grant its request.

27. Lord, forgive me,
and bless him forever:
exalt the high rank
of Your Prophet!

From His inspiration upon her concerning realization (43/125):

1. He who tastes the love of God vanishes
   from his selfish soul and its cares to abide in Him,

2. Annihilated without an eye or trace remaining,
   rapt in witnessing the awesome beauty of His love.

3. All of his fanciful desires pass away
   in preference for what comes from his beloved.

4. He regards His prohibition as the greatest gift,
   and so, too, banishment from being near Him.

5. Vision of Him leads the lover to melt away
   as the epiphany refines him.

And from His inspiration upon her with a sudden thought (43/125):

If the Lord is pleased to give me grace
and bring my heart to the station of nearness,
Then I'll say good-bye to this world and its comforts,
and to all the good things of Paradise, too.

And from His inspiration upon her in a mystical state (*ḥāl*) (43/126):

I have nothing to do with sleep
as the dear ones have arrived
close to the presence,
drawing near the Lord of Power.
For if they leave me behind,
I will have no way or means
to take me
to their exalted station.

From His inspiration upon her (45/128):

Do not belittle a tear drop falling
from crying and weeping in fear of God,
For many oceans must burn with Hell-fire
to quench it and wash away so many sins.

From His inspiration upon her concerning the rules for recollection (*dhikr*) (51/136):

> You seeking all the rules for recollection of the Master,
> take them from me:
> Fear, and hope in tears, and remorse,
> purity, fidelity, and standing before His door with humility.

And similarly (51/136):

> You who recollects his Lord, recollection has conditions,
> and, my brother, inspiration depends on them:
> Humility and modesty, weeping and remorse,
> hope, and fear without despair.

And similarly (52/137):

> All the rules of recollection, I will tell you,
> so listen up, act on them, and achieve success:
> Permission, humility, hope, shame, and fear,
> truthfulness, presence, purity, fidelity, and flowing tears.

From His inspiration upon her after His blessings had wafted in (52/137-38):

1. When a breeze of acceptance wafts in,
   a deep love reminds me of union's covenant,

2. And when a flash of inspiration appears in my heart
   from my Lord, my eyes cloud up and pour.

3. When the leader calls out His name
   as the caravan departs, desire wants my heart to stay,

4. And when passion's fire is kindled in my ribs,
   I have sips of pure wine from recollection's cups.

5. If critics belittle my claims to love,
   well, my tale of love for Him is old,

6. And when others slander me because of Him,
   my every limb opposes them with passion.

7. If all the world abandons me,
   memory of Him remains my heart's close friend.

8. When the One I love is pleased, He guides me
   to the path of righteousness, the straight path,

9. And He brings me to the pastures of acceptance
   and gives me a taste of inspiration's fruitful knowledge.

10. He gives me a drink from the spring of love,
    and I attain what I seek and desire,

11. And He leads me to smell a scent on the breeze of nearness,
    reviving me, though the hot winds blow.

12. He tears away the veil of pride and heedlessness
    that cloud the skies of the heart,

13. So I behold the truth of *Truth* in every atom,
    and leave aside what passes and does not last.

14. O, Lord, confirm my view of You, for You are, indeed,
most generous with grace, all-knowing of needs![4]

4. In v. 13 of this poem, ᶜĀ'ishah again refers to Qur'ān 55:26-27: "All things on earth are passing away (*fānin*), while the majestic and beneficent countenance of your Lord abides (*yabqā*)."

From His inspiration upon her during a session of mystical audition (*samāᶜ*) (56/142-43):

1. Recollection of Him was sweet to taste
   when He whispered to my heart,

2. And his herald proclaimed:
   "Come quickly to me, obedient to Him!

3. "Arise, and enter Our presence
   with sincerity as We have ordered;

4. "Kneel before Our might and submit,
   and this will please Him.

5. "Give up everything
   until you see only Him,

6. "For one who comes before Our presence
   with what you have, We have remembered him.

7. "We accept him, for after the break,
   We mend it with happiness.

8. "Just so, after rejection,
   We confer nearness.

9. "What is trustworthy, We have attained;
   what is hoped for, He gives!"

10. My heart replied with obedience:
    "Your wish is my command!"

11. So He befriended my heart, then made it expand.
    He summoned it, then whispered to it lovingly.

12. He astonished it, then gave it comfort;
    annihilated it, then made it stay.

13. He made it his drinking-mate, then exalted it;
    He graced it and then was satisfied.

14. He made my heart present, then led it away;
    He gave it a drink and quenched it,

15. And He made it drunk, then baffled it;
    He revived it and gave it new life,

16. With a cup whose content
    was beyond the mind's grasp.

17. For the cup held "God!
    There is no deity but Him!"[5]

---

5. In v. 17, "God! There is no deity but Him," resonates with the first portion of Muslim profession of faith, *lā ilāha illā-llāh*, " There is no deity but God," a declaration that ᶜĀ'ishah believed to be one of the most efficacious formula for meditation, recollection (*dhikr*), and sessions of mystical audition (*samāᶜ*).

From His inspiration upon her (57/143):

> An hour of union with him,
> with his beauty unveiled,
> Brings the heart everything
> it ever wished for.

And from His inspiration upon her, a secret prayer (57/144):

1. You, One, encompassing His worshippers with His grace,
   All-Powerful, conquering the world with His might,

2. You, Who the cosmos declares to be
   unique, eternal, free of temporality,

3. With noble invocation of You, my life was sweet,
   and my heart strolled in beautiful gardens.

4. So, the heart fears only You, how can it fear others,
   when Your name, my God, is its refuge?

5. My heart has loved You madly since You revealed
   love's secret and made the heart a sign of love.

From His inspiration upon her (76-77/167-68):

1. Every mystical *state* changes,
   that is none of my concern,

2. And if it becomes a *station*,
   my Lord, I fear its cure.

3. Yet, if You decree a portion of it
   for me to bear,

4. My job will be to meet it
   face to face with all my care.

5. You are my desire, nothing else,
   for the heart is happy with You.

6. If one day that heart turns,
   it bends away from any other,

7. So that it may keep on
   in pursuit of You, my Lord,

8. And if nothing bars its way,
   the heart will never find trouble.

9. For if You continue to grant grace,
   my Master, the heart will be pure.

10. My critic argued against You,
    misleading with his loathing,

11. Telling me to forget You,
    as he carried on and lied.

12. How can he put out the light of the word
    that Your grace made a shining *lamp*

13. Within a heart whose way to You
    and crown, You made:

14. The gnostic, the beloved axis
    who beheld the Essence and Its face,

15. Whose bounty is from the emanation
    of the Prophet, whose light effaces night,

16. The best of creation, and the brightest lamp
    and light among humanity.

17. My Lord, bless him,
    and my masters, his gateway,

18. As long as morning bright
    delights us with dawn.[6]

---

6. In v. 12, ᶜĀ'ishah alludes to revelation, which the Qur'ān likens to "a shining light" (*nūran mubīnan*, 4:174), brought by the prophet Muhammad, who the Qur'ān calls "a shining lamp" (*sirāj munīr*: 33:46).

Also from [His inspiration] on a theme (84-85/177-78):

1. O King of the realm and its subjects,
   You are the furthest wish,
   the aim and the goal.

2. Rapture and longing,
   love, desire, and passion
   were imposed on your servant,

3. For reason was denied the Lord of *beauty*
   and forbidden from union
   with the Lord of *power* and *glory*.

4. Now, faith can not be repealed;
   rejection and avoidance
   were not prescribed to love.

5. Yet separation fanned the flames,
   and passion blazed up
   and made loving eyes sleepless.

6. The state of loss was clear,
   and the lover was exposed
   to wasting away and rapture.

7. Keep Your promise, my love,
   with sweet union
   with You alone, my joy,

8. You Who are all of me,
   my Lord and my holy day,
   fulfilling my pledge with a drink

9. From the spring of nearness, Beloved,
   in the cups of union
   and the vision of oneness,

10. With the Essence, with holiness,
    with perfection, with grace,
    with beauty, with intensity!

11. Come to me,
    grant me my wish, and clear away
    the clouds of separation and rejection

12. With the glory of Your chosen one,
    the beloved Prophet,
    the best of those who praised You,

13. Your special one, the pure,
    the merciful and generous,
    You, the noblest in giving what's needed.

14. Bless him and give him peace
    as long as You, love,
    always keep Your promise.

Emanations of Grace

From His inspiration upon her as an appeal for aid (90-91/184-85):

1. Love of my heart, give me
   everlasting attraction to You.

2. Efface my *essence* in Your essence
   and my attributes in Your's.

3. God, let my share of You
   be life with You, my Lord.

4. Make nearness my abode
   and draw me close to You, step by step.

5. Let me abide in You
   that I may be among Your beauties.

6. My Lord, guide to my heart
   the gifts of Your breeze,

7. And revive my spirit
   with Your unending sweet scents.

8. Polish my heart with an epiphany
   raising me to Your sublimity,

9. And care for the chosen Prophet, the crown
   of the family providing water at Mecca.

10. May my beloved guide, my exemplar,
    the axis of Your saints, command

11. Me to be quenched with the wine of love,
    for I am one of Your thirsty ones,

12. And to continue to bring Your gifts
    to me and my son.

13. Assist us always, God,
    with Your blessings,

14. And bless the most honored servant
    who effaced his essence in Your's,

15. So he saw Your essence, truly,
    while hearing Your words.

16. My Lord, bless him
    with Your everlasting blessings,

17. And all the prophets
    who drew near Your presence,

18. And bless the Prophet's family and companions,
    who were among Your greatest gifts.

19. Bless my guide and crown,
    and all of Your saints,

20. And bless every seeker
    standing before Your door,

21. That You will give the heart its desire
    of everlasting attraction to You.

22. When my heart whispers intimately to You,
    then I will have my wish of life with You![7]

---

7. In verse 9 of this poem, ᶜĀ'ishah refers to the prophet Muhammad's grandfather, ᶜAbd al-Muṭṭalib who, according to tradition, dug the well of Zamzam, located in the sacred precinct near the Kaᶜbah at Mecca. This, in turn, gave Muhammad's tribe of the Quraysh the privilege of giving water to the pilgrims there. For more details see Ibn Isḥāq, *The Life of Muhammad*, translated by A. Guillaume (Oxford, 1955), 62-64.

From His inspiration upon her in a sudden intimation (*fī wārid*) (105/199):

1. When I sought union with the one I love,
   His majesty replied that there was no path to Him.

2. So, I closed my eyes that had tried so hard to see Him,
   while in my heart, desire burned with separation's fire.

3. I was about to meet my death, when He was kind,
   and sweetly spoke to my heart, saying:

4. "If you want union from Us, be true to Us,
   set aside all else, strive for Us, and be humble.

5. "Leave yourself and come to Us with Our true love and grace.
   Make that your means to Me.

6. "Draw near Us, be devoted to Us; don't fear rejection.
   Turn toward a sacred precinct filled with acceptance.

7. "There, you will find providence draws you to Us,
   bringing sweet union,

8. "And you will leave there all but Us
   and appear in a station where true men alight.

9. "You will behold lights of power, and in their intensity,
   the shadow of difference will go and disappear.

10. "You will pass away, nothing to preserve you save Our *splendor*,
    as you behold, truly, the climax of desire.

11. "Then you will abide with Us, Our servant,
    pure, chosen by Us for Our secrets forever!"[8]

---

8. In this and several other poems, ᶜĀ'ishah follows the Qur'ān in depicting God as the Lord of the Worlds, who speaks with the royal "We," as in 50:38: "We created the heavens and the earth and what lies between . . . "

From His inspiration upon her (127-28/224-25):

1. You effaced me in *awe*
   until vanquished, I vanished,

2. And this brought Your *beauty*,
   until You restored me in grace.

3. If not for You, I would have no existence,
   and my fate would be nothingness.

4. Yet, I am happy, my spirit refreshed,
   for among the atoms, I won a drop of life.

5. In You is my hope and joy,
   so what despair if my Friend avoids me!

6. You, most high, Who lifts and cheers me,
   delight and preserve me, You, my obsession.

7. God, my Lord, kindly guided me,
   so misfortunes cleared away,

8. And He sent His Prophet in whom
   I have glory and grace, for he is my life!

9. May he receive from his Lord,
   prayers that will erase all my sins.

10. May He bless his family, companions, and helpers,
    the spiritual masters and their dependents,

11. As long as blossoms in the meadows smile in delight
    when the early clouds break down and cry,

12. As long as the dawn of nearness arises
    and nothing remains of the long night alone.

From His inspiration upon her, indicating His blessing her with her exemplary faith (163/263):

I have a Lord who rules the noble ones, those foremost in faith,
and deals, as He sees fit, with their states.
I sought refuge in Him when my heart was afraid,
and then, as God willed, I was in the safest place.

And on the same subject (163/263):

You are the *imām* from whom I never ask a favor
save I receive more than I had hoped,
And whenever I seek safety from what frightens me,
God's protection comes at once.

And from [His inspiration upon her] (164/265):

Desire and patience: the first conquers; the other is conquered.
Love and the heart: the first plunders; the other is plundered.
Rapture and reason: the first loots; the other is looted.
Passion and the lover: the first comes calling; the other accepts.

And from [His inspiration upon her] (165/267):

Whenever I am called to the taverns he readied for me,
and I see the cups of union he prepared for me,
Then he grants and fulfills my heart's desire,
and revives with drink what was dead in me.

And from [His inspiration upon her] (166/268):

Whenever the lover is deep in passion,
his eyes are blind to all but his love.
Then he sees nothing at all but his beloved
in whatever comes his way.

And from [His inspiration upon her] (167/269):

By Your essence, attributes and names,
Lord, You, my furthest desire,
Grant me a grace effacing me in You
where I will abide forever.

From His inspiration upon her (195-96/299-301):

1. My worries must have relief;
   my heart must have its joys.

2. My anxiety must have release;
   my fate must have its course.

3. My branch must have its fruit;
   my fragrance must be sweet.

4. My gardens must have blossoms;
   my house must have a roof.

5. My sadness must have mirth;
   my being must have fatigue.

6. My horizon must have moons;
   my lightning must scintillate.

7. My full moon must be bright;
   my morning must have dawn.

8. My affairs must have prosperity;
   my seas must have great depth.

9. My spirit must have proximity;
   my night must have its stars.

10. My being must have happiness;
    my voice must have a song.

11. My union must have rejoicing;
    my recollection must be devout.

12. My heart must have assistance;
    my grace must come in waves.

13. My separation must have union;
    my sun must set in splendor.

14. My veils must have one who rends them;
 he is the axis with rank on high,

15. My guide, my treasure, my stairs to the sky,
 my union, my hope, my goal, my relief,

16. Religion's beauty, Ismāʿīl al-Ḥawwārī,
 the magnificent, beneficent with bounty.

17. Gift from God, our Master, you, axis of God,
 set straight my crooked ways,

18. And with splendid aid, dispel the blindness from my heart
 that I might behold my enlightenment.

19. Fill the cup to the brim,
 and reveal its joyous sight,

20. And let me have it, you, my support,
 until I have quenched the fire within.

21. With inspiration, dispel the heart's stuffiness
 and help it to find the sweet scent.

22. Set my spirit free to roam,
 and grant me relief to drive away my distress.

23. Give your unceasing aid to me and your servant,
 my son, and cure my lameness.

24. Seek for me from the Beloved
 permission to bring me near by grace.

25. Intercede for me with Him, by His permission,
 for my furthest wish and clear vision.

26. O, axis, secure acceptance for me, a humble servant,
 and for my son, and bring back my joy.

27. Beseech for us your guiding light,
 the Prophet, to bring us ample aid.

28. O, axis, seek his intercession,
    as long as eyes behold the beautiful vision,

29. And seek your Master's blessing upon him,
    with prayers that will lift distress,

30. And blessings upon those with revelation,
    and the Prophet's family and noble companions,

31. And upon all of the masters and their followers,
    and may prayers come to your spirit, O axis,

32. As long as you kindly keep your pledge to a yearning one,
    that he be pure and see, and be rescued and saved![9]

---

9. In v. 10 of this poem ᶜĀ'ishah says: "my voice must have a song." The word translated as "song," *hazaj*, is also the name of an Arabic meter, and so this line might also be translated as "my voice must have meter," which is quite apt when speaking of ᶜĀ'ishah's poetry.

Emanations of Grace

From His inspiration upon her as a lamentation to Him (218/326):

1. Parting hurt me; the separation grows long.
   I am rejected, my wish denied.

2. I cannot lie down on my bed.
   My eyes are lined with sleeplessness.

3. What life do I have if his rejection lasts?
   I am done with life, even the life Hereafter.

4. For I am sure there can be no happy life for me
   unless union returns.

5. Sickness is my companion now
   since it entered my limbs and reached my heart.

6. Passion's flame will not go out
   until nearness returns from afar,

7. And my heart cries out having attained
   the grace it sought from the generous Lord;

8. "The pain is gone and we have attained our desires,
   with nothing more to ask for!"

From His inspiration upon her (233/343):

1. You, the essence of my essence, source of my character,
   secret of my actions, light of my enlightenment,

2. God, God, my being,
   You are never hidden from my sight!

3. How could You hide when You
   are the life of my spirit in every way?

4. You made my love come true, and renewed my rapture
   with the grace of beauty and beautiful grace.

5. I have no art save passing away;
   I have no quality save being pure.

6. Love of my heart, look upon me
   with the favor of union and the union of favor.

7. I see You clearly in the beauty of every perfection,
   in every grace, in every pure wine,

8. For You are always before my eyes
   in every look and glance.

9. You kept me safe in promised union,
   accepted and fulfilled.

10. So, You are, my Lord, in every rose;
    You are my fragrance from every sweet scent.

11. You are the sun with which I rise;
    You are the full moon before whom I stand.

12. You are kind to me in every endeavor,
    and You are my end in every kindness.

13. You are my revelation in every state;
    You are my state in every revelation.

14. You are the inner meaning of my intoxication,
    for without You, my sipping pure wine would not be sweet,

15. And how could that be, love of my heart,
    when sipping wine is my sweetest cure?

16. You are my dearest beloved,
    and You provide the purest wine.

17. You are the meaning at the source of all meanings,
    and You are never hidden from my sight!

From His inspiration upon her [a *muwashshaḥ*] (253-54/365-66):

I see no one but my love, when I'm here or when I'm gone.
  I see him always with me, for he's my destiny.

  O my joy and happiness,
    faithful love has graced me
  With passing away in abiding
    and abiding in passing away,
  With my reunion, my departure,
    and departure, my reunion.

So my heart, take pleasure, in union with my love;
  I see him always with me, for he's my destiny.

  He's my attributes, my essence;
    I see him and nothing more;
  He's my effacement, my endurance
    when I pass and then return.
  He's my union and dissolution
    in my aim and way of life;

He's my substance and my meaning, far away or near.
  I see him always with me, for he's my destiny.

  So by God, my heart, enjoy,
    for God made my bliss complete.
  I loved my lover and my lord,
    spring of my soul and being.
  Life, then, was good, for I was always near,
    as God made my vision last.

His brilliant flash, no other, appeared to me so clear.
  I see him always with me, for he's my destiny.

  My love was sweet, my rending fine,
    in love with beauty's lord.
  My union came, division left,
    my wide expansion stayed.
  My illusion gone, my truth proved true
    and unadorned appeared.

A handsome moon beguiled me; he held all wondrous things.
    I see him always with me, for he's my destiny.

By my life, I do intend
  he be my highest aim.
My art is passing away in him,
  passion, my food and drink.
He's my reason, my religion,
  my doctrine and devotion.

Wherever I turn my face, I see him alone, no other.
    I see him always with me, for he's my destiny![10]

---

10. In this poem, a *muwashshaḥ*, ᶜĀ'ishah suggests the holy nature of her love with several possible allusions to the prophet Muhammad, as she likens her lover (*ḥabīb*, v. 1), to the full moon (*badr*, v. 41); these are standard poetic references to Muhammad, the "beloved of God," whose face shone like the full moon. Moreover, ᶜĀ'ishah's refrain: *kayfa lā ashhaduhu* ("I see him always with me," or "How can I not see him;" v. 3ff.), may also be translated as "How can I not bear witness to him," echoing the Muslim profession of faith: *ashhadu an lā ilāha illā Allāha wa ashhadu anna Muḥammada rasūlu Allāh*, "I bear witness that there is no deity but God and I bear witness that Muhammad is the apostle of God." In the final verse, ᶜĀ'ishah alludes to Qur'ān 2:115, often quoted by Sufis: "Wherever you turn, there is the face (*wajh*) of God."

Emanations of Grace

From His inspiration upon her (264-65/377-79):

1. The sun and moon appeared on the horizon of my spirit,
   and the heart beheld what eyes could not see,

2. And sheer beauty revealed itself in its guises
   to insight's clear vision.

3. He is the lover, and in the sun of His oneness,
   difference disappeared without a trace of shadow.

4. He appeared to my eyes in a revelation,
   whose climax took my hand as the veils fell away.

5. Kindly, He did away with the distance between us,
   so there was no separation, no difference, no fickle fate,

6. And He bestowed effacement in Him and annihilation in abiding,
   though He remains forever bright and pure.

7. I behold beauty with eyes lined by His light,
   and His splendor was the eyes' sight.

8. My love's beauty is my vision, His presence my gardens,
   and their fruit is His love talk devoted to me.

9. My heart, take joy in union and its pleasures,
   for they are pure and fine.

10. My heart, there is nothing left for you to seek,
    no goal or end, save your fidelity.

11. These are the promised gardens whose gates
    open onto everlasting happiness.

12. This is the tavern of joy where the glasses are full,
    aglow like the sun and moon.

13. These choice cups are a portion of what comes to me
    as their quiet intimacy takes hold.

14. This is the wine of leisure, and I received from it
    perfect fulfillment from an endless source,

15. A wine taking me to the fountain of bliss,
    as I attained peace without anxiety or fear,

16. And I won there an intimacy, so near,
    beyond imagining, as my heart had hoped.

17. My expansion stayed with my intoxication there,
    and I heard nothing of coming down or sobering up.

18. After that, there is nothing left for me to seek,
    nothing left to wish or wait for.

19. I found all I sought there,
    and my victory was true as He promised.

20. My mind, my spirit, my faith—all of me
    sees clearly without a veil or screen.

21. So I received the greatest joy and wish,
    and grace to me is limitless.

22. My spirit is my love; I live in Him forever,
    with my full union set, never to come undone.

23. Exhilaration is my state, and joys are doubled for me,
    for depression is repressed and expansion set free.

24. God is great! For there is no rejection after fulfillment,
    and there is no need, after one attains the ultimate aim![11]

---

11. In this poem, ᶜĀ'ishah contrasts the limited range of oracular sight (*baṣar*; v. 1), with the penetrating vision of mystical insight (*baṣā'r*; v. 2). Further, the "ultimate aim" (*al-muntahā*; v. 2) for which she aspires may be the beatific vision that Muhammad beheld by the "furthest lote tree" (*sidrati-l-muntahā*; Q. 53:14). God has promised the beatific vision to believers in the gardens of Paradise, to which ᶜĀ'ishah alludes in v. 11. In v. 22, ᶜĀ'ishah puns on terms for poetry (*naẓm*) and prose (*nathr*) when she says: "with my full union set (*naẓm*), never to come undone (*yantathiru*)."

From God's inspiration upon her in a *takhmīs* ("quintain") on the ode by the savior, the unique axis, my master ᶜAbd al-Qādir al-Jīlānī, may the high God sanctify his heart and may we benefit from him! (290-92/406-407):

In the garden of union, I praised my love,
I saw rare beauty, and was rapt in delight.
As the server came round, I drank and sang:

1. *There is no source of honeyed drink,*
save mine is more tasty and sweet.

There is no perfection of note or dignity
save it was fixed to my deeds
and related in my beautiful words.

2. *The most perfect union is a special place,*
yet my station is more awesome and near.

There, I tamed my selfish soul with its effacement.
Then, His cups came full to me,
and I was among their intoxicating bouquets.

3. *Time gave me its pure splendid drink*
whose source was pleasant, its taste sweet.

My nature in love was purified by a sign
wiping away all misfortune
and revealing to my heart the greatest gift.

4. *So I was called to every honor*
that the mind had never seen nor sought!

I am among the nobles whose selfish souls have passed away,
abiding in Him Who is their intimate in fidelity,
and in the tavern of His presence, He sent their cups around.

5. *I am among men who do not fear the change of time*
and who are afraid of nothing.

Outstanding, powerful, prime, elite,
energetic, noble, chosen, beloved,
brave men, freeborn, special, bonded together:

6. *A folk who have a high place in all glory,*
and who are the vanguard of every army.

Secrets of my union are impossible to tell,
though I've read what their tablets contain.
So my allusions are for those who breathe their scent.

7. *I am the nightingale of mirth, filling its branches with song,*
while high above, I am the grey falcon in the sky.

Since my effort was true in effacing my being
and the True Beloved cleared away the shadow of "me,"
I stayed in the Eternal without plurality.

8. *The troops of love fell under my will, willingly,*
and whatever I desired, I captured.

When He gave me the drink of oneness,
I was drunk with contemplation's drunkenness,
and I attained my ends in union.

9. *I began to hope, but without desire or expectation,*
anticipating no promised thing.

I continued to be drawn, moving freely in space,
as my annihilation led me to pure excitement.
Yet, when I desired to describe it, I could only use allusion.

10. *I continued to revel in the square of acceptance,*
until I was given a rank never bestowed before.

How many promised gifts
have we bestowed to the elite we know,
when we governed them with authority.

11. *Then time was like royal vestments, patterned and bright,*
while we were their trim of gold.

We are those who, if one turns to us as our intimate disciple,
he will look and behold our holiness,
as revelations of awe and brilliance call him!

12. *May the suns of the forefathers and our sun*
ever travel in the highest heaven and never set.[12]

12. In this *takhmīs*, ᶜĀ'ishah precedes each verse of ᶜAbd al-Qādir's poem (= 2 stanzas) with three stanzas of her own in elaboration and/or commentary (3 stanzas + 2 stanzas = 5 = a *takkhmīs*/quintain).

From His inspiration upon her (294-96/411-14): [13]

You who annihilates mystically
those absorbed in love of You,
Give to me! Give to me!
Grant me a good life and immortality
with clear vision in union.

Yā Hū, yā Hū, yā Allāh, yā Hū, yā Hū, yā Allāh, yā Hū, yā Hū, yā Allāh
Yā Allāh, yā Hū, yā Allāh!

My love, my desire,
my goal, my being
Be mine! Be mine!
And mend my break and free me from poverty
with nearness and union.

Yā Hū, yā Hū, yā Allāh, yā Hū, yā Hū, yā Allāh, yā Hū, yā Hū, yā Allāh
Yā Allāh, yā Hū, yā Allāh!

Love of You bereaved one who loves You:
I was dazed when I lost
My reason, my reason,
And love bewildered me and kept me up all night
as it led me on and wore me out.

Yā Hū, yā Hū, yā Allāh, yā Hū, yā Hū, yā Allāh, yā Hū, yā Hū, yā Allāh
Yā Allāh, yā Hū, yā Allāh!

---

13. This poem is a *muwashshaḥ* in which ᶜĀ'ishah repeats the refrain: *Yā Hū, yā Hū, yā Allāh,* "O Him, O Him, O God!" The terms *hū* ("him") and *Allāh* ("God") are often used in Sufi recitation practice (*dhikr*), and I have retained the Arabic refrain to give an idea of the rhythm of the poem, which ᶜĀ'ishah may have composed as a Sufi chant. As is the case in her other *muwashshaḥ*, ᶜĀ'ishah often leaves aside the rules of formal Arabic in order to maintain vowel harmony and the beat of her poem. In stanza six, ᶜĀ'ishah says: "In His epiphany, when He called out from His brilliant fire." This is a reference to the story of Moses and his encounter with the Burning Bush as recounted in the Qur'ān 27:7-11.

Emanations of Grace

Your beauty bound me tight,
and when the light appeared, gone was
My shadow, my shadow,
And it stripped me, and nothing remained with me,
as it annihilated me as was right.

Yā Hū, yā Hū, yā Allāh, yā Hū, yā Hū, yā Allāh, yā Hū, yā Hū, yā Allāh
Yā Allāh, yā Hū, yā Allāh!

I left myself and went away.
My veil was gone, and my nearness appeared
With my union, with my union!
For, He had astonished me, then revived me,
and He gave me new life in beauty.

Yā Hū, yā Hū, yā Allāh, yā Hū, yā Hū, yā Allāh, yā Hū, yā Hū, yā Allāh
Yā Allāh, yā Hū, yā Allāh!

In His epiphany, when He called out
from His brilliant fire,
He said to me, He said to me:
"Arise, drink, and enjoy
the goodness of grace!"

Yā Hū, yā Hū, yā Allāh, yā Hū, yā Hū, yā Allāh, yā Hū, yā Hū, yā Allāh
Yā Allāh, yā Hū, yā Allāh!

For He had set out for me a radiant cup
filled for me with the pure wine of truth.
He gave to me, He gave to me
This pure drink with relief,
and hope and peace.

Yā Hū, yā Hū, yā Allāh, yā Hū, yā Hū, yā Allāh, yā Hū, yā Hū, yā Allāh
Yā Allāh, yā Hū, yā Allāh!

These jars of wine are unveiled gifts
of gnosis to their tavern-mates,
My folk, my folk,
My masters, my loves,
my brothers in my mystical states.

Emanations of Grace

Yā Hū, yā Hū, yā Allāh, yā Hū, yā Hū, yā Allāh, yā Hū, yā Hū, yā Allāh
Yā Allāh, yā Hū, yā Allāh!

I have an exalted axis among them
who appeared with his fidelity
To me, to me,
And he drew me and brought me near
and raised me up in nobility.

Yā Hū, yā Hū, yā Allāh, yā Hū, yā Hū, yā Allāh, yā Hū, yā Hū, yā Allāh
Yā Allāh, yā Hū, yā Allāh!

My Master, the greatest to come among us
is the most exalted Prophet.
Bless him, bless him!
And all the apostles, his family
and closest friends, You Most High!

Yā Hū, yā Hū, yā Allāh, yā Hū, yā Hū, yā Allāh, yā Hū, yā Hū, yā Allāh
Yā Allāh, yā Hū, yā Allāh!

As long as Your cup comes to my heart
with Your wine in the tavern of nearness
As my drink, as my drink,
Given to me to drink, quenching me,
and reviving me in union!

Yā Hū, yā Hū, yā Allāh, yā Hū, yā Hū, yā Allāh, yā Hū, yā Hū, yā Allāh
Yā Allāh, yā Hū, yā Allāh!

From God's inspiration upon her in the form of the master to his disciple [here named Sa^{c}d] (298-99/415-17):

1. Union, with its peaks,
   no one knows its meaning
   save a hero annihilated,
   with nothing left behind.

2. This gnostic knows for sure
   the Real's splendor in the heart
   where he is always free:
   only he knows union.

3. He suffered to disappear in love,
   so he was drawn to Him,
   and then his being was plundered
   when He preserved him in union.

4. If you seek union, Sa^{c}d,
   then become a suitor,
   for you must pass away
   to meet Him in union!

5. You will have good fortune, Sa^{c}d,
   with ample aid and grace,
   if the Generous is generous to you
   revealing the sense of union.

6. If He calls you, Sa'd, rejoice,
   for He has brought you near.
   If you can leave yourself behind,
   you will abide in union.

7. But he who blames and demeans it
   is godless and never grows,
   for the Real is the revealer,
   and God is God!

8. Yet were He to bless the forsaken
   with release from fate's decree,
   they would not deny this light
   nor the special friends of union.

9. Those who rule are masters
   surpassing one and all,
      and in the tavern halls, they are revived
   by the wine of union.

10. So the folk are drunk on it
   with the secret suddenly revealed
      when it was seen in secret
   by the intimates of union.

11. These tavern-mates are heroes,
   with true gnosis of Him,
      and hidden from all creation
   when union's face appeared.

12. What comes next in this affair
   is a question for His lovers,
      so give up this ignorant "other,"
   and attain the vision of union!

From His inspiration upon her (300-301/418-19):

1. My love, you are near my heart,
   your beauty ever present within me.

2. You bestowed loveliness in self-revealing robes,
   and I beheld beauty no one else saw.

3. You made union last forever;
   there was no turning back, no suspicion or doubt.

4. In concord's tavern, you passed round to me
   a cup whose taste made life sweet

5. With a wine quenching all thirst
   as divine secrets took shape before me.

6. Drunk, I rose to a station where
   wondrous powers were given to me,

7. As my shadows vanished with the rising of my sun;
   it appeared but never set,

8. And I arrived in a courtyard with you there,
   my destiny, love of my heart.

9. You drink with me and ply me with wine;
   you take me to you, so I will never go.

10. You bring me close to behold
    a beauty sacred, without equal.

11. So there is no fear, for you guard my heart;
    there is no illness, save you are the cure.

12. There is no sorrow with your joy within my heart,
    and there is no doubt you are my love!

13. This is the farthest hope of the seeker,
    hidden senses whose study is rare,

14. And this quest, this goal, this is the aim
    of the chosen ones and those given power.

15. This intimacy, this exhilaration,
    is pure of any taint, immaculate;

16. This emanation, this grace,
    is the awesome gift and blessing.

17. How many souls have died in love with him;
    how many hearts have melted in him!

18. You who seeks him with a love that's true,
    if you are truly wise,

19. Strip away yourself, leave yourself, and go to him,
    and you will see him near, indeed.

20. So win your goal from him; shoot your arrows true,
    and hit the mark to pass away in him.

From His inspiration upon her (310-11/430-31):

1. These are the gardens of eternity,
   fulfilling what was promised.

2. They were opened wide,
   and the Beloved's beauty appeared there.

3. He said: "O woman whose existence
   was consumed in mine,

4. "I have preserved you in Me forever
   as My generous gift.

5. "So you are living in Me,
   summoned to witness Me.

6. "So behold and enjoy
   without limits or bounds,

7. "In the shade of the manna tree
   protected from ruckus and rejection.

8. "Before you is a wine unveiled
   in the tavern of good fortunes.

9. "It quenches the thirsty, so enjoy it
   with its sweet bouquet,

10. "Without anyone sober there,
    blaming with slander.

11. "Kindly give the thirsty ones a drink
    from My shower of generous gifts.

12. "For I have fulfilled My promises
    as I have kept My covenants!

13. "As a servant, you have pleased Me,
    and for service, I grant authority.

14. "So I made you a leader
    among My troops and armies

15. "To bear witness and confide
    and be graced by My presence.

16. "Those I accept, you will guide;
    those I reject, you will drive away,

17. "And you will praise finding Me,
    in these gardens of eternity!"[14]

14. Once again, ᶜĀ'ishah alludes to the gardens of Paradise and the beatific vision that will be had there. The word for "beloved" in this poem is *Wadūd*, one of God's ninety-nine Beautiful Names. For more on these names, see L. Gardet, "*Al-Asmā' al-Ḥusnā*," in the *Encyclopaedia of Islam*, 2nd ed., 1:714-17.

From the high God's inspiration upon her (321-22/442-43):

1. My love kindly called me to the tavern,
   and with grace, he passed round a full cup.

2. He singled out my heart for his pure wine,
   and a fine charming man came forth.

3. Since he appeared, I have passed away
   from my being, my existence, and all else,

4. And in my passing was my perfect abiding in union,
   so I was an eye witnessing the Merciful.

5. My love was my tavern mate, union with him, my fate,
   exhilaration my state, the tavern my public place.

6. Intimacy was my mezze; the singer was my wine,
   and a gentle whisper with my love was sweet-scented basil.

7. My wine revealed my heart's companion without a veil,
   and His folk were the brothers.

8. All you seeking Him, make pilgrimage to me;
   hurry, as I have, until you fly.

9. Steel your will, self-sacrifice is due;
   pass away completely and be the companions!

10. How many sleepless nights I passed in rapture,
    moaning and restless with sorrows,

11. Streaks of tears running down my cheeks,
    with love's fire burning in my ribs.

12. My rapture was intense; there was nothing I could do;
    patience was impossible, and solace had left.

13. There was no way to evade my flowing love,
    no second chance to leave my solitude.

14. Then, when He called me to Him, my heart cried out:
    "At Your service, Lord of the tavern mates!"

15. And I began to confide in Him, so near,
    and I was always with the Sultan.

16. In my annihilation and absence from me,
    my abiding remained in the garden of gnosis.

17. My life was sweet, my time refined,
    and my expansion stayed, as I was embraced with acceptance.

18. I had no want after this fulfillment,
    no separation after union.

19. So cheers to you, heart, be happy and cheerful,
    and live in delight with His glass that is full!

From the high God's inspiration upon her (335-36/459-61):[15]

1. Sufis, to the tavern!
   The kind God will serve you, now!
   Lose yourselves in Him, erase all else,
   and He will keep you there as friends.

2. Sufis, the filter has clarified the wine
   the server provides as He wills,
   and one blessed with the wine rejoices
   in the presence of this merciful Lord.

3. Sufis, this is a wine
   whose tavern is the presence divine,
   and a drop of it the dead revives
   with its sublime intoxication.

4. Sufis, purify your hearts
   of sediments from seeing others,
   and He will grant your every wish
   and quench all who thirst.

5. Sufis, one who comes courting,
   desiring this wine, let that seeker
   give his spirit as a dowry
   and annihilate the rest.

6. Sufis, go, go to the tavern!
   Hurry! Hurry!
   Leave nothing of you behind,
   and He will quench you in the gardens with wine.

7. Sufis, annihilate sensation
   with the cup's clear wine.
   One tasting it among the folk is refined,
   while the Sultan is flush with wine.

15. This is the final poem in ᶜĀ'ishah's *Emanation of Grace and the Gathering Union.*

8. It can bring certain knowledge;
it's of the highest quality;
and it has the meaning to the secret
of changing shapes before the eyes.

9. In it, letting go is easy;
with it, comes success;
from it, one is realized:
God's people, be preserved with this!

10. People of God, assist your God.
Servants strive for God,
and their hands, Sufis, reach out for aid.
Give to them, you folk of faith.

11. You, who are the secret of happiness,
I have only you, my patrons.
Help me with assistance
and give me the grace of gnosis.

12. The servant has only his Lord;
how many God has drawn to Him.
He gave to them till they were content,
and He revived them with a cup that's full.

13. The lover has only the beloved;
from Your grace, he wins rewards,
and from Your gift, he attains the goal
from the pure wine of the Beneficent.

14. The wine of His became my lot in life,
its drink became my trace;
all my knowledge, I drew from wine,
as it gave me the exalted sign.

15. For my heart, its tavern is Paradise,
its unveiling, the Ka^{c}bah of my being;
its server is God, my Lord,
so I'm completely drunk with wine.

16. You, seeking this exhilaration,
    arise and untie the wraps;
    ask Him, and receive your rapture,
    and attain the pure delight.

17. In my passing away, I follow
    in my shade with my worthy masters,
    in bliss before the Essence,
    in the presence of gnosis and truth.[16]

---

16. This poem is a *kān wa-kān*, in which each Arabic verse consists of four hemistiches, the first three of which rhyme, while the fourth bears the end rhyme of the poem consisting of a long vowel followed by a consonant: e.g., nnnān, bbbān, cccān, etc. The *kān wa-kān* became popular in the 7th/13th century, especially for sermons and giving religious advice, as in this poem..

Ode in “T” (*al-Tā’īyah al-Bāʿūnīyah*)

by

ʿĀ’ishah al-Bāʿūnīyah

From His inspiration upon her concerning various mystical stations (139-51/237-51):

1. He quenched me with love's heady wine
before my birth,
and I delighted in my drunk
prior to my being,

2. And he called me to witness beauty's grace
as He willed what He desired
when He willed
my bearing witness,

3. And He placed in my heart
the joy of a secret
beyond the grasp
of insight or understanding,

4. Exalted, high above
phenomenon's embrace,
awesome, beyond
the understanding of man or beast!

5. He made me hear His call
whose melody
is well beyond the harmony
of any kind of words,

6. A call to Him
that I desire still,
as I urge my heart and soul
to hear it,

7. Saying: "Perhaps this
will lead to a recovery
and sooth my sorrows."
Yet, my love pangs sharpen.

8. In the mosque of love and passion,
He made me call to prayer
impassioned lovers,
the worthy ones of love.

9. "O legists of love,
I have disappeared in love
where 'I' is effaced
in the essence of 'Him.'

10. "There is no wrong
in the passing of plurality,
dignity, and passion
to please the beloved."

11. They replied: "In recollecting the beloved
there is a refreshing pause for breath."
They spoke true,
yet my flowing passion rises.

12. So my state when speaking
is the desperate love to mention Him,
while my state in silence
is bewildered awe.

13. I brush aside my blamers
when they gather in ignorance
to blame me,
and I refute them with that.

14. They say: "You don't listen!"
So I turn a deaf ear
that makes them choke
on their bitter rage.

15. They ask: "Who do you love?"
I reply: "What is love?"
"So many secrets!" they reply,
Yet my words are telling.

16. So if you are like me in love,
you hero,
then be completely
bound by beauty.

17. Before you is my way.
  So advance onward, as I have done.
    Don't fear those who mock you;
      stand firm!

18. Love of Him called me,
  so I answered with all of me
    annihilated within
      His everlasting essence.

19. So I cried: "Here I am Lord!"
  in annihilation from all else,
    as my intention to perform the pilgrimage
      was the passing of my human nature.

20. And on the *ᶜArafāt* of love,
  I stood in a station
    that every weak seeker
      had yet to reach.

21. And from there the departure
  was only to a presence,
    holy, undefiled
      by how or why.

22. And in the oasis of *Minā*,
  I attained the desires there
    in a union without separation
      by the wish of my desired one.

23. I slaughtered my selfish soul
  against its wishes,
    so He delivered it
      from every evil and temptation.

24. My heart remained
  with providence as my mount
    traveling to the *Door of Peace*
      pulled by my *attraction*.

25. Then my heart circled beauty's fine favors
praying to the awesome glory
of the Essence
without a veil,

26. And grace was my *Ṣafā'*,
intimacy my *Marwah*,
and the running there
gave thanks to the law of love.

27. My way was annihilation in Him,
as I was shorn of everything,
for limitation
is bound to my clay.

28. He caressed my heart
when the pilgrim rites were through,
and from His high call,
I waxed full of grace.

29. How very fine,
a mystical Hajj,
fulfilling my *ᶜUmrah*
with my bond and my fate.

30. There I drank a sip
from the *Zamzam* well of love
that cured me of every illness
and disease within.

31. I stood there
beneath the *Spout of His blessings*,
and as it flowed freely,
I attained what I needed most.

32. Before His door, I made my heart
wallow in the dust,
while the place for prayer
was in a holy presence.

33. Then after the Hajj,
people have a most noble custom:
visiting the tomb of the *Hashimite*,
my intercessor.

34. So on this Hajj, my heart
paid a visit to his heart,
and I gave it the utmost desire
and greatest wish.

35. And by the grace of God,
the flood of His blessing returned,
and all of my worlds
savored it.

36. For to God belongs all who exalt Him
on a sacred pilgrimage
with which my spirit won
the highest bliss!

37. You who struggles
with love,
if you want to follow me,
then choose my way of life,

38. And seek out
a clear exposition of my school.
Here are its principles;
grasp them firmly:

39. My annihilation is in my love.
My abiding is in His light.
My humiliation is my exaltation,
and my abasement is my high station.

40. My distress is my comfort.
My need is my wealth.
My death is my life,
and my contrition is my cheer.

41. I regard prohibition as an offering,
rejection as acceptance,
my distance as nearness,
and my fracture as my being set firm.

42. And when it was clear to insight
that all reality
is passing and vain
save my Beloved,

43. And that there is nothing save His essence,
His attributes, and actions,
with all else
but traces of His power--

44. For one does not win acceptance
by obedience
nor is one driven out by sin.
No. It is by divine will.

45. Indeed, the actions of creation
are His creation, too,
and created things do not control
an atom's weight of their affair--

46. Then all save Him vanished
in my mystical vision,
and I saw nothing but Him
with the eye of truth!

47. But after I performed my rite
by His grace,
I felt that I
had given in to sin.

48. For while I stood before God,
I fell short
considering my delusion
that I had something of obedience.

49. But because He is with me,
  I have never turned away from guidance
    as I carry out my duty on the straight path
      with my sound tradition.

50. Yet no time passed for me
  free of sin,
    as there was no obedience
      save it held a slippery evil.

51. For there is no good
  not tainted with evil,
    nor any goal
      not caused by weakness.

52. There is no speaking
  without complaints to be clear,
    nor any action
      that comes without error.

53. But my heart so full of sin
  trusts in Him
    for a forgiveness
      that will clear my many sins away.

54. If one day He grants
  a drop from His heaven,
    I am absolutely sure
      that it will sink in.

55. So when sins weigh down my back
  and I fear and dread them,
    then hope for forgiveness comes to my mind,
      and my sins grow light and disappear.

56. How can I fear sin
  or be deprived of grace
    when I have in beautiful forgiveness
      the loveliest design?

57. How can I imagine that obedience is mine
when it is His grace?
For His gift
is not by my power or strength!

58. Acts of kindness flowed from Him,
and they were glad tidings
coming within mystical meanings
intimating:

59. The attainment of my goal
and the gaining of my wish,
the realization of my hope,
and the raising of my rank,

60. And a joining without parting,
a closeness without distance,
a giving without forbidding,
and a generosity with union,

61. An expansion without contraction,
comfort without disquiet,
grace without fear,
and blessings of kindness,

62. An illumination without a veil,
love without hate,
union without severance,
and the seclusion of the bridal chamber,

63. And a cup, I know not how,
and a filtered wine
in an earthen jar close by,
opened in the tavern of love,

64. Filled with care
and passed round
fragrant with wine,
soothing with rest.

65. A life-giving cup reviving every heart
with its bouquet,
quenching and annihilating its drinker
in His essence.

66. They say: "Describe the wine
and its effects to us;
speak clearly
and dispel the taint of doubt."

67. So I replied:
"Were its luster to appear at night,
then pitch black would turn
to brightest noon,

68. "And if infidels could smell
the sweet scent of its bouquet,
they would submit
to the Muslim creed,

69. "And if one whose illness
was beyond the doctors' cure
could taste its blend,
that blend would restore his health.

70. "Were that pure wine
sprinkled straight on a dead man,
by the grace of God,
he would quickly rise alive!

71. "It dispels blindness and quenches thirst;
it enters the sanctuary
and brings health,
driving out cares with delight.

72. "It removes harm as it gives right guidance;
it subdues the foe and dispels debility,
and it contains my greatest goals,
the aim of my desire.

73. "It banishes ignorance; it gives gifts;
it pardons error and brings contentment
as it puts out the fire
of every dispute.

74. "It dispels antipathy and guides to felicity;
it requires fidelity
as it lifts you up
to meet the beloveds.

75. "It leads to nobility; it bestows loyalty;
it confers clarity
and nurtures intelligence,
guiding beauty with tranquility.

76. "It is the sun
save it never sets,
while it casts those worthy of wine
into the desert of concealment.

77. "The full moon its glass,
and stars are its bubbles,
while the tavern-mates are the dear ones,
the worthy folk of love.

78. "And its tavern is holy,
everlasting,
free of the impurities
of size or shape.

79. "And the All-Merciful,
exalted is His glory,
bestows it directly as a grace
on whom He wills.

80. "There was never a day
when its fragrant bouquet
spread through the mind
without it guiding to the mystic path,

81. "And since time began,
its luster never shone
to mystic vision
without guiding to the truth,

82. "And the heart
never tasted it
without the clouds of God's grace
drawing near and pouring down,

83. "And the spirit
never tasted it
without blessings flowing to it
with joys of delight,

84. "And the heart secret
never tasted it
without the clouds of separation parting
to reveal the sun of union."

85. So if the wine wishes,
I will sit and drink with its loveliness
giving it my spirit,
spending freely with my being.

86. Then how heavy will be my scale,
how gainful my trade,
how sweet my transactions,
how great my worth!

87. "Depart now, my sadness,
while my happiness, you stay;
O, my delight, be glad,
and may my joy last forever!"

88. How could I forget it
when I was predisposed
to love it
before the leavening of my clay?

89. To renounce it would shame me
since we have covenants
between us that we keep
in compliance with love.

90. With His blessings,
God's providence preserved it
from loss and oblivion
in every case.

91. I was crazed by it
until I was thrown into madness,
and my mania was my passion
for Paradise.

92. So the selfish soul could not recall it
without anxiety,
while the spirit could not remember it
without longing.

93. My heart burns
in the fire of passionate love,
yet were it to forget its rapture,
it could not be consoled!

94. But I did not forget my intimacy
when I saw the wine's light
on a mountain of enlightenment
where I had no time for thought,

95. Where it whispered to me
of a grace
confirming my salvation
from evil and temptation.

96. When the blessing appeared
that I had sought,
I saw the mountain of being
crumble away from me,

97. And the Moses hidden in my heart
was struck by an awesome thunderbolt
which, if not for beauty,
would have destroyed him.

98. Then, by beautiful grace,
he awoke in mercy,
turning again and again to glorify God
after repenting.

99. So this is my story
on the love of wine,
the best of charms for one
bitten by the vipers of love.

100. Love of wine effaced me,
though it left a little behind;
had it pitied my condition,
it would have destroyed the rest of me.

101. What could be said of me
save that the passing existence of "I"
passed away
in the everlasting essence of "Him,"

102. And the one with me in this
is my utmost desire,
the Ka'bah of my hopes,
and the Medina of my goodness!

103. But my blamers say:
"Savor something else."
But were I to listen to them,
I would lose my religion.

104. Should I bear witness to something else
after seeing its loveliness?
By my life, that would be obvious
ignorance and heedlessness.

105. If I wanted to abstain from it,
that would be hard to do,
and solace for it too, is rare,
even if I tried.

106. For it is my craving;
in it is my rapture;
from it is my infamy,
for I long for it in extreme.

107. If those visiting me in my illness
grow weary, well, my selfish soul
was used to my sickness,
as if it no longer cared.

108. And if the slanderer spreads his tale
that I think no more of wine,
the clear proof of my state and shape
show him to be a liar.

109. With it, I abstained from me,
and I fell in love,
guarding it jealously
lest thought of it fly by.

110. I entered its precinct
and held fast to its rope.
How wondrous:
my shelter is a garden!

111. I was crazed for it,
so when I heard it mentioned,
my every atom and iota
gave praise.

112. I was nourished with it
in the world of atoms
as I grew dizzy, intoxicated,
drinking it at the beginning of my being.

113. You coward to commitment,
  how long will you lay claim to passion?
    For you have yet to meet
      even one of love's conditions,

114. Since we were called
  to pass away in our beloved
    by the summons of him
      who quickly reached Him first,

115. Who clears away from you
  the dust of delusion
    so that you may behold the beloved
      when annihilation comes with life,

116. An annihilation, by my life,
  leading to the courtyard of abiding,
    without passing away
      or a cutting rapture,

117. A path to the spring of life,
  and from its water
    the green meadow of hearts
      comes alive with a sip.

118. I savored the intimacy of passion
  in love with Him in whom
    I found passing away
      to truly be the sweetest pleasure.

119. Existence is always absolved there
  if one comes seeking
    annihilation in Him
      with resolve and a firm desire.

120. I exhaust my energy
  seeking out union with Him,
    but providence comes
      and revives my resolve.

121. I fear for my peace of mind
from the power of His possession,
yet due to my zeal, He awakens in me
an exciting rapture.

122. So when a glorious flash appeared
from the awesome mountain side,
it leveled and annihilated
my existence,

123. And then came my resurrection
with a beautiful breath
that bestowed blessings,
brought life, and revived me.

124. How wondrous my state
from end to beginning!
How wondrous my death
and new life in love!

125. From life and death,
I arose with a drunken spirit;
how lovely my birth,
how sweet my intoxication!

126. It would be best for you to turn with me
to the mountain of His affection,
to the right of the oasis of love
in the best of places.

127. For I have a mystical tale
about its lofty places
that threw the Arabic of intellect
into the maze of my gibberish.

128. Yet my critics abused me
and oppressed me with blame,
though had they turned to excuse me,
they would have won my company.

129. I surpassed them in refinement,
so they had no way to ascend
from the lowlands of the selfish soul
to the lofty peaks above.

130. If only that state of mine
had been their state,
then the unadorned among them
would have been bedecked with silence.

131. Well, to Hell with them!
How they tried to move me with blame,
yet in love with my lover
I hold firm.

132. They want me to stay away
from my love,
Him to whom I'm driven
for He created my spark.

133. How long can I mislead
those empty folk
and guard the passion in my heart
when my state tells my story?

134. It is love
exposing every slave to passion;
just so, the dazzling road
runs to God.

135. So leave the path
of those empty of passion,
and turn with me to Him
for that is the way of my faith.

136. I never turned away from Him,
no, nor did I ever leave Him
after I settled in Him,
though my selfish soul took no delight in that.

137. By Him, my moment was pure,
and my watering places ran clear;
my words were subtle,
and my allusions refined.

138. So glad tidings came to me
while my troubles turned away;
my joys were sweet,
delighting me with union.

139. My zephyr was fresh,
and my gatherings a delight;
my morning dawned bright
as my veil of night fell away,

140. And my branch bore fruit;
my planets shone;
my full moon appeared,
then my sun rose clear.

141. And my sweet basil was brought
and my sweets were served;
the cups of wine went round
in the very best presence,

142. And my existence vanished completely
in my contemplation,
blessed at last
with my final, greatest goal!

143. So this is the life
that I have loved so much
and that made me reside
in the nest of passion.

144. My critics' opinions
were divided on me
for they did not know
my luck with good fortune.

145. For I pledged my allegiance
  to the Sultan of love and passion,
    effacing all of me in Him,
      spending me all away.

146. So I hope for providence
  from my Beloved's generosity
    to fulfill the terms
      of my pledge to love Him.

147. Man of rapture,
  leave one empty of love,
    one so ignorant of the beloved
      and blind to a lovely sight,

148. And follow one who sold
  his selfish soul for love
    for an hour of union
      with my beloveds,

149. Who met love's terms
  in word and deed,
    who never wavered
      in doing his duty,

150. Who never failed to carry out
  what was required of him
    by the law
      of love's religion.

151. The power of glory
  refined him with its awe;
    the subtlety of beauty
      polished him with mercy,

152. And he became worthy
  of contemplation,
    a bearer of generosity,
      and a secret place for every grace,

153. And he was brought near
and entrusted, ascending close;
he was purified, made sincere,
and chosen for sainthood.

154. He was greeted and given life,
pleased with His call;
he was watered and quenched
from the pure pools of love.

155. He was adorned
as the wraps of his veils were removed,
and he was blessed with the union
of union without parting.

156. The command from his Lord's decree
arose from him
and was made firm in this
by the strongest strength.

157. And on the horizons, he was made to summon
in the name of his ascension,
the saints of the time
from every direction.

158. So all of existence was entrusted
with the legacy of him
who has the right to be called "the axis,"
as well as my exemplar,

159. My imam,
the beauty of truth and religion,
the guide named Ismāʿīl,
the exalted one of the mystic way,

160. My leader in my seeking
my way to desires,
my lamp in my darkness,
my help in my troubled times,

161. My guide to my happiness,
 my glory among humanity,
  my master in the law
   of guidance and truth,

162. The providence of My Master,
 the favor of my Lord,
  long granted
   prior to the creation of my form,

163. The light of my sight,
 pupil of my eye of insight,
  my advocate for attaining the goal,
   my means

164. To the best of creation,
 the noblest intercessor,
  the most exalted of those
   chosen for the secret of love,

165. The most awesome envoy,
 the most excellent one
  sent with the straightest path
   to the best community,

166. A prophet who has
 in the presence of proximity
  a rank above
   every favored companion,

167. A beloved for whom
 my Lord created existing things,
  so he became the spirit of the cosmos
   and the secret of the universe.

168. A dear friend who gave up everything
 but Him, as was fit,
  for the All-Merciful befriended him
   with the most awesome friendship,

169. A glorious one who God--
how great is His glory--
robed with a splendor
that all glories glorified,

170. A handsome one with whom
God beautified His creation,
bringing him forth
as protector and mercy for me.

171. He created him
the peak of epiphany,
the manifest authority,
and a grace, my greatest blessing,

172. A welcome sea
of overflowing grace,
as all other things
draw their drink from him,

173. A land for the greatest gathering
of piety for the pious,
as he became the goal
of pious people everywhere,

174. A sun whose full splendor
is by the light of lights,
from whom all other lights
borrow without doubt,

175. A full moon close on the horizon,
whole and shining still
without waning
or a veil of clouds,

176. A secret to whom the elite
turn their hearts in prayer;
a mystical sense, like the Ka^{c}bah
for the lords of mysteries.

177. God bestowed upon him
  what He gave all the prophets,
    but he was selected for other things
      beyond measure.

178. So when I was oppressed
  by my existence and self-regard,
    and by my confinement
      in the cellars of my concealment,

179. And the diseases were strange,
  their remedies rare,
    and I saw no way out
      of my predicament,

180. Then the providence of God
  led me to his door,
    and I said: "I entrust
      my poverty and sorrow to him!"

181. Apostle of God,
  I have been inspired
    to seek refuge in your cave
      with humility as my adornment.

182. Apostle of God,
  I was granted a grace
    to lay down my needs
      and story before you.

183. Apostle of God,
  I have no means save you
    for mercy for my spirit
      and the rest of me.

184. Apostle of God,
  I cannot draw near Him
    save by belief in oneness,
      and my love.

185. Apostle of God,
my firm faith is in Him
as to what holds
the supreme knowledge of His essence.

186. Apostle of God,
I believe in one who came from Him
bringing word of Him
in a book and sound tradition.

187. Apostle of God,
I loved everyone He loved,
and I met the enemies
with my enmity.

188. Apostle of God,
all my merits are from Him,
while from me
is only the shame of sin.

189. Apostle of God,
all my sins are met
and turned away
by the gift of forgiveness.

190. Apostle of God,
I was made to bear witness
to His grace for me
in good times or bad.

191. Apostle of God,
everything is a gift from God,
not from my effort
or ability.

192. Apostle of God,
when I wish to give thanks for it,
I see that too is a gift,
so I confess my lowly state.

193. Apostle of God,
  you are my means;
    Apostle of God,
      you are my treasure.

194. Apostle of God,
  you are my sure remedy
    for recovery
      from all illness.

195. Apostle of God,
  you are my shining guide
    to salvation
      from error and oppression.

196. Apostle of God,
  you are my safe haven,
    high above
      strife and affliction.

197. Apostle of God,
  you quench me
    with the purest drink
      from the wine of love.

198. Apostle of God,
  among all creation
    you are the dearest love
      to my heart.

199. Apostle of God,
  I have nothing to offer
    save sincerity
      in my love and affection for you.

200. Apostle of God,
  I have no support
    save you
      when my case confounds me.

201. Apostle of God,
  I have no help
    save you
      when my distress disables me.

202. Apostle of God,
  separation takes away my reason,
    casting my thoughts
      into the ocean of my confusion.

203. Apostle of God,
  rejection will cloud my days
    and cover my life
      with dust.

204. Apostle of God,
  the fire of desire
    melted the heart within me
      as my tears flowed.

205. Apostle of God,
  long have I lingered
    in the prison of my exile
      without attaining my desire.

206. Apostle of God,
  I need a remedy to cure me,
    so grant me the cure
      with my return.

207. Apostle of God,
  if I should die
    before attaining my desire,
      then how great my pain, how long my grief!

208. Apostle of God,
  if you will not help me
    with your rank, my Prophet,
      then I will perish in my obscurity.

209. Apostle of God,
if you would cast a glance
at my sinful soul,
it would be at rest.

210. Apostle of God,
my poverty is real,
but if you are generous to me,
you will enrich me with the best of riches!

211. Apostle of God,
far be it from you to deny
one hoping for your blessing,
the best of gifts.

212. Apostle of God,
how often equality is bestowed with union,
yet my way station
is in the prison of rejection.

213. Apostle of God,
if it would please you
that I be among the servants,
then how great will be my glory!

214. Apostle of God,
unite me in a union
full of my share of you,
granting my desire.

215. Apostle of God,
give it all to me
in an emanation
spreading the secret in every instant.

216. Apostle of God,
give me a glance
that will make me worthy
for the pull of oneness.

217. Apostle of God,
  all of me thirsts
    for one holy
      and everlasting drink.

218. Apostle of God,
  one who has you for his support
    is triumphant
      like the mighty victors.

219. Apostle of God,
  one who has you for his glory
    is the sultan
      among all creation.

220. Apostle of God,
  one who has you for his refuge
    is saved
      without a shadow of a doubt.

221. Apostle of God,
  one who has you for his treasure
    is rich
      in any state or circumstance.

222. Apostle of God,
  one who has you for his intercessor
    attains his hopes
      as quick as a flash!

223. Apostle of God,
  blessing to humanity,
    best creation,
      and the best of means,

224. Best of those who intercede,
  whose intercession
    is always welcomed,
      best support of all creation,

225. I sought you, my Prophet,
for intercession with God,
my Compassionate One,
who was merciful to my lowly state

226. With the realization of my hopes,
the attainment of my aims,
and reaching my desires
to the furthest degree,

227. By removing my cares,
and clearing my clouds away,
as I attained the union of union
without separation,

228. As I was drawn to Him
and was refreshed by His nearness,
as I drank
from the pure wine of love,

229. Face to face as required
in the seat of truth
in contemplation
free of any veil!

230. May God bless you
with His purest prayers,
may He give you, my Prophet,
the supreme life,

231. With prayers preserved by God
in abundant clouds
and sent with glad tidings
of attaining the means,

232. With prayers that content you
as you intercede for me
and all the lovers
with the Master's acceptance,

233. With prayers that attain the goal
from the emanation of His grace
providing salvation, with God's help,
from temptation,

234. And may He bless your brothers,
the masters,
whose full moons shone
on the horizon of prophecy,

235. And then the Truthful One,
the first male believer,
and after the Apostle of God,
the greatest caliph,

236. And then him who became most excellent
in telling right from wrong
with recollection
and sound tradition,

237. And then him who gathered
all of His book
and equipped God's army
in troubled times,

238. And then the Sword of God
who has the power
on the *Day of Reward*
to raise the banner high.

239. Then may God bless
the group of Ten Noble Ones,
and Hamzah, and 'Abbas
who was asked for water in creation,

240. And may He bless with every sacrifice,
the Apostle's two grandsons,
his noble kin and companions,
his wives and family,

241. And those who walk behind them
in knowledge, forbearance, and guidance,
following them
in every act and intention,

242. And the special ones
chosen for His love,
and their axes
in every clime and country,

243. And their axis al-Jīlī,
my imam, in whose lofty heights
the poles were established,
one and all!

244. Then may God bless my guide,
my crown and my way,
my treasure, glory and support
among my folk,

245. My imam, the axis of the age,
Ismāᶜīl, whose full moon
rose high on the horizon
of the knowledge of reality!

246. May the clouds
of God's mercy
continue to shower them
with favor and long life,

247. And grant each of them
their every wish,
and grant me my wish
and utmost desire,

248. And may His mercy
encompass along with them,
our parents and family,
and all who protect them in creation.

249. As long as the flowers
of the meadow exude
their sweet scent inhaled
from a dear passing zephyr,

250. As long as the verdant meadow
smiles in wonder
as the clouds break down
and cry at dawn,

251. As long as the sincere seeker
gains his hope
and loses his cares
in union with the beloveds,

252. And as long as the first pledge of fidelity
is recited among the noble ones:
"I drank the heady wine of love
before my birth!"

Homage to Ibn al-Fāriḍ: A Commentary on ᶜĀ'ishah al-Bāᶜūnīyah's "Ode in T"

ᶜĀ'ishah al-Bāᶜūnīyah consciously modeled her longest poem rhyming in the letter "t" on verse by the famous Sufi poet ᶜUmar Ibn al-Fāriḍ (d. 632/1235). Ibn al-Fāriḍ lived most of his life in Cairo where he taught the traditions of the prophet Muhammad (*ḥadīth*), and composed and taught poetry. After Ibn al-Fāriḍ died, his grandson, ᶜAlī (fl. 735/1334) collected this verse, to which he added a reverential account of his grandfather, including tales of mystical states and miracles. By ᶜĀ'ishah's day, Ibn al-Fāriḍ was regarded as one of the great saints of Cairo, and his verse was enormously popular.[1] Perhaps his most celebrated poem is the *Naẓm al-Sulūk* ("Poem of the Sufi Way"), often referred to as the *al-Tā'īyah al-Kubrā* ("Ode in T – Major").[2] This poem is one of the longest in Arabic, spanning 760 verses, as Ibn al-Fāriḍ speaks of love, the mystic quest, and spiritual intoxication, which culminate in an experience of union during the Hajj pilgrimage at the sacred precinct in Mecca. Not surprisingly, then, when ᶜĀ'ishah al-Bāᶜūnīyah composed her own poem on Islamic mysticism, she chose to imitate Ibn al-Fāriḍ's *al-Tā'īyah al-Kubrā*, which begins in praise of wine and the beloved:

saqatnī ḥumayyā-l-ḥubbi rāḥatu muqlatī
wa-ka'sī muḥayyā man ᶜani-l-ḥusni jallati[3]

The palm of my eye handed me
love's heady wine to drink,
and my glass was a face
of one revealing loveliness.

Drunk by my glance, I caused
my companions to suppose
that drinking their wine
had brought my heart joy.

---

1. See Th. Emil Homerin, *From Arab Poet to Muslim Saint: Ibn Fāriḍ, His Verse and His Shrine*, 2nd ed. (Cairo, 2001).

2. See Th. Emil Homerin, *ᶜUmar Ibn al-Fāriḍ: Sufi Verse, Saintly Life* (New York, 2001), 67-291, for an annotated English translation of the poem.

3. Ibn al-Fāriḍ, *Dīwān Ibn al-Fāriḍ*, ed. Guiseppe Scattolin (Cairo, 2004), 66.

But by the dark pupils of the eyes
I did without my drinking bowl;
from the fine qualities of eyes, not cold wine,
came my intoxication.

ᶜĀ'ishah signals her debt to Ibn al-Fāriḍ's poem in her own opening verses using the same rhyme, meter and similar images:

saqānī ḥumayyā-l-ḥubbi min qabli nash'atī
min qabli wujdānī ṭaribtu bi-nashwatī

He quenched me with love's heady wine
before my birth,
and I delighted in my drunk
prior to my being,

And he called me to witness beauty's grace
as He willed what He desired
when He willed
my bearing witness,

And He placed in my heart
the joy of a secret
beyond the grasp
of insight or understanding.

Whereas both poems begin as wine odes, Ibn al-Fāriḍ's *al-Tā'īyah al-Kubrā* quickly veers away from wine to speak of love and a woman, who comes to represent the divine beloved, encountered during the pilgrimage in Mecca (vv. 148-53):

In truth, I led my prayer leader in prayer
with humanity behind me;
wherever I turned
was my way,

And my eyes saw her before me
in my prayer,
my heart witnessing me
leading all my leaders.

It is no wonder
that the prayer leader prayed toward me
since she had settled in my heart,
as niche of my prayer niche.

All six directions faced me
with all there was
of piety and pilgrimage
both great (*ḥajj*) and small (*ᶜumrah*).

To her I prayed my prayers
at Abraham's station,
while I witnessed in them
that she did pray to me:

Both of us one worshipper
bowing to his reality
in union
in every prostration.

Ultimately, this experience leads the mystic back to the Day of the Covenant (vv. 155-64) to which Ibn al-Fāriḍ returns later in the poem (vv. 354-73).

ᶜĀ'ishah leaves no doubt as to her male lover's identity as God, who called forth the spirits of humanity in pre-eternity to take the covenant from them (vv. 1-5). For both ᶜĀ'ishah and Ibn al-Fāriḍ, this initial meeting leads to love of God and a longing to be in His presence once again. For Ibn al-Fāriḍ (vv. 430-41) and ᶜĀ'ishah (v. 11), this may be achieved through recollection (*dhikr*), and divine grace. ᶜĀ'ishah dismisses her critics who can not fathom her abiding love, which annihilates her selfish will in union with God (vv. 15-18). She then assumes the role of the spiritual master, as Ibn al-Fāriḍ often does, to recall a moment of union as embodied in the Hajj pilgrimage. ᶜĀ'ishah names various places and rituals of the pilgrimage and alludes to their spiritual significance: the plain of ᶜArafāt, where pilgrims stand in prayer, is the station of gnosis (*ᶜarafah*); the oasis of Minā where the sacrifice is made, becomes the site of sacrificing her selfish soul to attain her desire (*muná*) for union, while the water from the well of Zamzam, represents love that can cure all things. With these and other specific references, ᶜĀ'ishah constructs an elaborate mystical allegory involving not only the Hajj (*ḥijjah maᶜnawīyah*; v. 29), but also the ᶜUmrah or "lesser pilgrimage," and the subsequent visitation (*ziyārah*) of the Prophet's mosque in Medina (vv. 19-36).[4]

---

4. Regarding pilgrimage in Islam, see G.E. Von Grunebaum, *Muhammadan Festivals* (New York, 1951), 15-49.

After recounting this mystical event, ᶜĀ'ishah, like Ibn al-Fāriḍ, resumes the role of the mystical guide. While Ibn al-Fāriḍ spreads his teachings over scores of verses (e.g., vv. 164-241), ᶜĀ'ishah is fairly terse regarding the importance of annihilation and abiding, obedience and poverty (vv. 37-41). Both mystics conclude that only God truly exists, and here ᶜĀ'ishah has several verses that clearly resonate with the teachings of ᶜAbd al-Qādir al-Jīlānī (d. 561/1166), the founder of the Sufi order to which she belonged (vv. 44-45):

For one does not win acceptance
by obedience
nor is one driven out by sin.
No. It is by divine will.

Indeed, the actions of creation
are His creation, too,
and created things do not control
an atom's weight of their affair.

In one of his sermons, ᶜAbd al-Qādir al-Jīlānī said:

> Human actions and their consequences are the creation of God, the great and glorious. God, most high, has said [Q. 16:32]: "Enter the Garden for what you have done!" Glory be to Him! How generous and merciful is He! He attributes to them acts that entitle them to enter Paradise, yet this is only due to His help and mercy in this world and the Hereafter. The Prophet, may God bless him and give him peace, said: "No one enters Paradise due to his own action." It was said to him: "Not even you, O Apostle of God?" "No, not even me, unless God encompasses me with His mercy!"[5]

Though God has blessed ᶜĀ'ishah with union, she suddenly feels guilty of spiritual pride. ᶜĀ'ishah thought that she had earned union through obedience, when her union was in fact an act of grace (vv. 47-55). While lamenting her mistake, ᶜĀ'ishah again follows in the footsteps of al-Jīlānī, as she takes solace in God's mercy and compassion and His granting her union, to which she turns again (vv. 56-62). Using an expression from Ibn al-Fāriḍ's *al-Tā'īyah al-Kubrā* (v. 6), ᶜĀ'ishah likens the experience of union to the wedding night alone with her love in the bridal chamber (*khalwati jalwah*; v. 62). There, they sip the wine of love, and, for this next

5. ᶜAbd al-Qādir al-Jīlānī, *Futūḥ al-Ghayb*, ed. Muhammad Sālim al-Bawwāb (Damascus, 1986), 49; my translation. For more on ᶜAbd al-Qādir al-Jīlānī see the *Encyclopaedia of Islam*, 2nd ed., 1:69-70 (W. Braune), and Alexander Knysh, *Islamic Mysticism: A Short Introduction* (Leiden, 2000), 179-83.

section, ᶜĀ'ishah draws from another famous poem by Ibn al-Fāriḍ, his *al-Khamrīyah*, or *Wine Ode*, in which he celebrates the eternal love between God and humanity:[6]

In memory of the beloved
we drank a wine;
we were drunk with it
before creation of the vine.

ᶜĀ'ishah alludes to this pre-eternal vintage in her opening verse when she says:

He quenched me with love's heady wine
before my birth,
and I delighted in my drunk
prior to my being.

Just as the poet is asked to describe the wine in Ibn al-Fāriḍ's *Wine Ode*, (v. 21), so too is ᶜĀ'ishah, who proceeds to enumerate the amazing appearance and powers of this celestial drink, which can illuminate the night, cure ills, and even raise the dead (vv. 66-81). ᶜĀ'ishah's account of the wine's miraculous effects parallels Ibn al-Fāriḍ's *Wine Ode*, (vv. 7-20), as does her description of the wine in its glass (76-77):

It is the sun
save it never sets,
while it casts those worthy of wine
into the desert of concealment.

The full moon its glass,
and stars are its bubbles,
while the tavern-mates are the dear ones,
the worthy folk of love.

Ibn al-Fāriḍ wrote (v. 2):

The full moon its glass, the wine
a sun circled by a crescent;
when it is mixed,
how many stars appear!

ᶜĀ'ishah explicitly links this wine with God's grace of love and mystical

6. Ibn al-Fāriḍ, *Dīwān*, 158-61. For a complete translation see *ᶜUmar Ibn Fāriḍ*, 41-51, and also see Th. Emil Homerin, *The Wine of Love and Life: Ibn Fāriḍ's al-Khamrīah and al-Qayṣarī's Quest for Meaning* (Chicago, 2005).

union, and she notes the wondrous effects that it has on her heart and spirit, as it leads her to recall a moment in pre-eternity (v. 88):

> How could I forget it
> when I was predisposed
> to love it
> before the leavening of my clay?

Similarly, Ibn al-Fāriḍ said (v. 27):

> While it made me drunk
> before my birth
> abiding always with me
> though my bones be worn away.

ᶜĀ'ishah next confesses that the wine has made her yearn for Paradise whose residents, according to Islamic doctrine, will drink wine and see the face of God. This, in turn, spurs ᶜĀ'ishah on to discipline her selfish soul (*nafs*), while her heart burns with love and her spirit longs to return to the divine presence (vv. 91-93). Nevertheless, she takes comfort in the knowledge of her ultimate salvation as she again recalls a powerful mystical experience. This time, however, ᶜĀ'ishah introduces a new allegory involving "the Moses hidden in my heart" (v. 97). In a Divine Saying popular among the Sufis, God says: "My earth and My heaven do not hold Me, but the heart of My believing servant holds Me." Sufis have interpreted this to mean that the heart is a place of mystical encounter between the mystic and God.[7] In her allegory, then, ᶜĀ'ishah likens her heart to Mt. Sinai where the prophet Moses spoke with God. According to the Qur'ān 7:143, while on Mt. Sinai, Moses asked to see God:

> When Moses arrived at the appointed time, and his Lord spoke with him, [Moses] said: "My Lord, reveal Yourself to me, that I might gaze upon You." He said: "You can not see Me! Rather, look upon the mountain. If it stays in place, you will see Me" Then, his Lord revealed Himself to the mountain; this leveled it, and Moses fell down, stunned. When he recovered, [Moses] said: "Glory be to You! I turn to You with repentance, and I am the foremost of believers!"

For ᶜĀ'ishah, Mt. Sinai stands for her heart where she received enlightenment and the grace of salvation. There, she lost herself in God, only to be revived to praise him (vv. 94-98). This story of Moses had long served as a mystical allegory for Sufis,[8] but ᶜĀ'ishah may have thought that she was drawing once

7. See Chittick, *Sufi Path*, 106-109.

8. See Annemarie Schimmel, *Mystical Dimensions of Islam* (Chapel Hill, NC, 1975), 43.

again on Ibn al-Fāriḍ's verse. For in his *Dīwān* is an appendix compiled by his grandson ᶜAli, containing poems that had either been ascribed to Ibn al-Fāriḍ by his companions or composed in imitation of his verse. By ᶜĀ'ishah's day, many believed that Ibn al-Fāriḍ had composed these poems, and in one of them, the poet assumes the role of the mystical Moses:[9]

When the appointed time
drew near for my union,
My mountain crumbled
in awe of the epiphany,
And there appeared a hidden secret
that only one like me knows,
And I became the Moses of my time,
as a part of me became my all.
So in death was my life,
and in my life was my death!

At this point, nearly half way through her poem, ᶜĀ'ishah appears to draw a section to a close (v. 99):

So this is my story
on the love of wine,
the best of charms for one
bitten by the vipers of love.

But she begins again to recall how her identity (*wujūdu anā*) was effaced in the "everlasting essence of Him" (*bāqī-l-huwīyati*, v. 101). To return to that moment is her greatest wish, and she is not to be put off by her critics (100-108). ᶜĀ'ishah again asserts that this love is her pre-eternal destiny, and she urges those who are afraid of commitment to follow the one who called them to annihilation in love, undoubtedly the prophet Muhammad, the first to attain this high station (vv. 112-115). Those who can follow his example will abide in rapture with their Lord, as ᶜĀ'ishah has done (vv. 119-120). Referring again to the story of Moses on Sinai, ᶜĀ'ishah describes her mystical experience as a blinding flash of awe that ended her life of ignorance and brought her to a new life of intoxicating love (vv. 121-26). Similar to Ibn al-Fāriḍ in his *al-Tā'īyah al-Kubrā* (e.g., vv. 475-93), ᶜĀ'ishah rejects her critics and affirms her own high status in gnosis (vv. 127-34), and she cites her personal experience of union as an example of a life of true passion free of selfishness. Her love of God has transformed her existence into one of joy and happiness, regardless of what her critics think (vv. 135-46),

9. Ibn al-Fārid, *Dīwān*, 230, vv. 9-13. Also see Th. Emil Homerin, "Ibn al-Fāriḍ's Personal *Dīwān*," in *Le développement du Soufisme en Égypte à l'èpoque mamelouke*, ed. Richard McGregor and Adam Sabra (Cairo, 2006), 233-43.

and so she urges others on to love and the beatific vision (v. 147):

Man of rapture,
leave one empty of love,
one so ignorant of the beloved
and blind to a lovely sight.

However, this verse is more than an exhortation to turn away from those who do not seek out love, as a closer look at the Arabic reveals:

akhā-l-wajdi da^c khālin mina-l-ḥubbi ^cammahu
^cammā-l-jahli bi-l-maḥbūbi ^can ḥusni rūyati

This is an instance of a word-play in Arabic is known as *tawrīyah* ("double entendre") or *īhām* ("making someone to imagine something else"). Here, ^cĀ'ishah uses the words *akhā* ("man," "companion"), *khālin* ("empty"), and *^camma* ("to consume totally," "to encompass everything"), while punning on their respective alternative meanings of "brother," "maternal uncle," and "paternal uncle." At first glance, then, one might read this verse as:

Brother of rapture, for love,
leave a maternal uncle whose paternal uncle
is so ignorant of the beloved
and blind to a lovely sight!

Not surprisingly, Ibn al-Fāriḍ had also made a similar double entendre using these and other terms in one his poems.[10]

With this rhetorical *tour de force* and yet another nod to Ibn al-Fāriḍ, ^cĀ'ishah concludes her account of love and union, and turns to praise. Long eulogies of the prophet Muhammad and other pious Muslims are common in ^cĀ'ishah's verse, but they are not found in Ibn al-Fāriḍ's poems, as such extensive verse in praise of the Prophet (*al-madīḥ al-nabawī*) only became a marked feature of Arabic poetry several generations after Ibn al-Fāriḍ's death in the 7th/13th century.[11] In this section, ^cĀ'ishah lauds her mystical guide (vv. 148-63), the saint and spiritual axis, Ismā^cīl al-Ḥawwārī, who was destined by God to be her guide since pre-eternity (v. 162). ^cĀ'ishah describes Ismā^cīl in the present tense, strongly suggesting that he was still alive when she composed this poem, which would then have been before

10. Ibn al-Fārid, *Dīwān*, 51, v. 18. Also see Al-Ḥasan al-Būrīnī, *Sharḥ Dīwān Sulṭān al-Āshiqīn Sayyidī ^cUmar Ibn al-Fāriḍ*, ed. Rushayyid ibn Ghālib al-Daḥdāḥ (Cairo, 1888), 1:91-94. For a study of *tawrīyah* and *īhām*, see S. A. Bonebakker, *Some Early Definitions of the Tawryia and Safadī's Fadd al-Xitām ^can at-Tawrīya wa'l-Istixdām* (The Hague, 1966).

11. Concerning Muslim belief in the power of blessings upon the prophet Muhammad to aid them, see Schimmel, *And Muhammad*, 92-104.

his death in 900/1495. ᶜĀ'ishah regards her teacher to be the spiritual heir to the prophet Muhammad, who is ᶜĀ'ishah's next subject of praise as the greatest prophet of God (vv. 164-77). As in many other poems, mention of Muhammad leads ᶜĀ'ishah to the topic of his intercession on behalf of Muslims (vv. 178-80):

So when I was oppressed
by my existence and self-regard,
and by my confinement
in the cellars of my concealment,

And the diseases were strange,
their remedies rare,
and I saw no way out
of my predicament,

Then the providence of God
led me to his door,
and I said: "I entrust
my poverty and sorrow to him!"

Then, ᶜĀ'ishah beseeches the Prophet for help over the next thirty-two verses, beginning each verse with: *a-lā yā rasūlu-llāh*, "O Apostle of God!" She begins by asking for refuge in the Prophet's cave, a reference to the place where, according to Muslim tradition, Muhammad hid to escape the Meccans who wanted to kill him in 622 CE.[12] ᶜĀ'ishah goes to on confess her sins and swear her fidelity to God and His prophet (181-223). Then, following this long petition for aid, ᶜĀ'ishah confirms that her request for intercession was, indeed, granted, leading to her mystical union (vv, 224-29):

Best of those who intercede,
whose intercession
is always welcomed,
best support of all creation,

I sought you, my Prophet,
for intercession with God,
my Compassionate One,
who was merciful to my lowly state

12. See, Schimmel, *And Muhammad*, 13.

With the realization of my hopes,
the attainment of my aims,
and reaching my desires
to the furthest degree,

By removing my cares,
and clearing my clouds away,
as I attained the union of union
without separation,

As I was drawn to Him
and was refreshed by His nearness,
as I drank
from the pure wine of love,

Face to face as required
in the seat of truth
in contemplation
free of any veil!

In an earlier poem in her *Emanation of Grace*, ᶜĀ'ishah noted that she had been inspired "as she stood before the Noble Stone," that is, before the Black Stone in the Kaᶜbah, during her pilgrimage to Mecca.[13] In that poem, as in her petition above, she was repentant and desperate, as she asked the prophet Muhammad to intercede for her. In another work praising Muhammad, ᶜĀ'ishah tells of an experience she had in Mecca, "when an anxiety had overcome me," which led her to dream of the Prophet:

> Then, I could not believe my eyes, for it was as if I was standing among a group of women. Someone said: "Kiss the Prophet!" and a dread came over me that made me swoon until the Prophet passed before me. Then I sought his intercession and, with a stammering tongue, I said to God's Messenger, "O my master, I ask you for intercession!" Then I heard him say calmly and deliberately, "I am the intercessor on the Judgment Day!"[14]

Read in context of these experiences, this section of her "Ode in T" may allude to ᶜĀ'ishah's salvation anxiety and dream in Mecca, which eventually resulted in union and a happy life. For, according to one tradition, Muhammad said: "Whosoever sees me in a dream has seen me in a waking state,

13. This poem is found on pg. 45 of the anthology.
14. For the full account, see the introduction.

for Satan cannot imitate me."[15] This popular tradition may well have led to ᶜĀ'ishah's belief in her own salvation and the beatific vision to come, of which she speaks in many of her later poems in the *Emanation of Grace*,[16] and which is clearly implied by her reference in the "Ode in T" to "the seat of truth" (v. 229). This phrase is used in Qur'ān 54:54-55 to describe the exalted state of those residents of Paradise who are near God: "As for the righteous, they are in gardens with streams, in a seat of truth (*fī maqᶜadi ṣidqin*) before a mighty King!"

ᶜĀ'ishah concludes her "Ode in T" with more blessings and prayers, first upon the Prophet Muhammad (vv. 230-33), and the other prophets (v. 234). Then, in a series of verses, she asks God to bless other major figures of early Muslim history, beginning with the first four caliphs to succeed Muhammad: the "truthful" Abū Bakr (d. 13/ 634), the moralist ᶜUmar ibn al-Khaṭṭāb (d. 23/644), ᶜUthman (d. 35/656), who had the Qur'ān collected, and, finally, Muhammad's cousin and son-in-law, the brave ᶜAlī (d. 40/661) the "Sword of Islam" (vv. 235-38), all of whom are also mentioned by Ibn al-Fāriḍ in his *al-Tā'īyah al-Kubrā* (vv. 619-25). Next, ᶜĀ'ishah asks God to bless the "Ten Noble Ones and Ḥamzah and ᶜAbbās" (v. 239). ᶜAbbās (d. 32/653) was Muhammad's uncle who was in charge of the sacred well of Zamzam, while Ḥamzah (d. 625), was another uncle noted for his bravery and killed fighting with Muhammad against the Meccans in the Battle of Uḥud. The "Ten Noble Ones" refers to ten of Muhammad's closet companions, including the first four caliphs, who were promised Paradise.[17] ᶜĀ'ishah then asks God to bless "the Apostle's two grandsons," who were the children of ᶜAlī and Muhammad's daughter Fāṭimah (d. 11/632), al-Ḥasan (d. 49/670), and al-Ḥusayn, from whom descended ᶜĀ'ishah's husband and son.[18] Finally, ᶜĀ'ishah asks God to bless the founder of her Sufi order and one of God's greatest saints, al-Jīlī, meaning ᶜAbd al-Qādir al-Jīlānī, and her spiritual guide, Ismāᶜīl al-Ḥawwārī (vv. 241-51). Then, she returns full circle, at the end, to her beginning and pre-eternity (v. 252):

> And as long as the first pledge of fidelity
> is recited among the noble ones:
> "I drank the heady wine of love
> before my birth!"

---

15. John C. Lamoreaux, *The Early Muslim Tradition of Dream Interpretation* (Albany, 2002), 32, and also see Schimmel, *And Muhammad*, 79-80.

16. E.g., the poem beginning: "These are the gardens of Eternity," in this anthology.

17. See the *Encyclopaedia of Islam*, 2nd ed. 1:9 (W.M.Watt), 3:152-54 (G.M. Meredith-Owens), and Schimmel, *And Muhammad*, 14, 22-23, 111, 268, n. 55.

18. See the *Encyclopaedia of Islam*, 2nd ed., 2:841-50; 3:240-43; 3:607-15 (L. Veccia Vaglieri).

Glossary

Abiding: *baqā'*, and related terms, signify the mystical state and/or station of being preserved in union with God after the annihilation of the mystic's selfish soul. This is the antonym of "annihilation" and "effacement."

Absence: *ghaybah*, and related terms, signify trance and the absence of ordinary consciousness in a transcendental state.

Annihilation: *fanā'*, and related terms, signify the loss of the mystic's selfish will and desires which are consumed in God's will. This is the complement of "abiding." Also see "soul."

ᶜArafāt: a plain about twelve miles southwest of Mecca where pilgrims gather during the pilgrimage to pray and declare their willingness to serve God. This occasion has been likened by Muslims to a preview of the Judgment Day. For Sufis, the name ᶜArafāt resonates with *ᶜarafah* and *ᶜirfān*, terms for gnosis. Also see "gnosis."

Attraction: *jadhb*, and related terms, signify God's drawing His worshipper to Him.

Audition: *samāᶜ*, listening to the Qur'ān, poetry, song, or chant for purposes of meditation and trance. Also see "recollection."

Axis: *quṭb*, a title of honor used by ᶜĀ'ishah for her spiritual master Jamāl al-Dīn Ismāᶜīl al-Ḥawwārī (d.900/1495). In Sufi circles, the "axis" often designates the most spiritually enlightened individual alive at any given time. Also see "savior."

Banner of Guidance: *ᶜalam al-hudā*, an epithet of the prophet Muhammad.

Banner of Praise: *liwā' al-ḥamd*, an epithet of the prophet Muhammad. According to tradition, on the Day of Judgment, Muhammad will hold this banner, under which the faithful will gather for his intercession with God on their behalf. Also see "intercession."

Beauty: ᶜĀ'ishah uses several terms that mean beauty, and one of them, *jamāl*, often designates one of God's attributes. Grace and acceptance flow from this attribute. *Jamāl* is the complement of *jalāl*, "glory" and "power."

Beloved: ᶜĀ'ishah uses several terms to designate the beloved. One of them, *Wadūd,* is among God's ninety-nine Beautiful Names.

Best of Creation: *khayr al-khalq*, an epithet of the prophet Muhammad.

Best of Humanity: *khayr al-wará*, an epithet of the prophet Muhammad.

Blamer: In classical Arabic poetry, the blamer, the slanderer, and the spy are characters who try to prevent the lover from being true to the beloved.

Chosen One: *al-muṣtfá*; *al-mukhtār*, an epithet of the prophet Muhammad.

Constriction: *qabḍ*, and related terms, signify spiritual and emotional states of dejection and depression. This is the antonym of "exhilaration" and "expansion."

Covenant: *ᶜahd*; *mīthāq*. In classical Arabic poetry, the covenant is the pledge of fidelity between the lover and the beloved. In addition, for ᶜĀ'ishah and other Sufis, this covenant also refers to the "Day of the Covenant" (*yawm al-mīthāq*) when the primordial bond between the human spirits and God was taken by Him in pre-eternity as suggested by Qur'ān 7:172. For more on this concept, see the introduction.

Critic: see "blamer."

Day of the Covenant: see "covenant."

Day of Reward: the Judgment Day. Also see "Banner of Praise."

Dhikr: see "recollection."

Dīwān: a collection of poetry, usually by a single author.

Door of Peace: *bāb al-salām*, the northern gate to the Great Mosque enclosing the Kaᶜbah in Mecca. Also see "Kaᶜbah" and "Mecca."

Ecstasy: *wajd*, *wujūd*, see "rapture."

Effacement: *maḥw*, and related terms, signify the loss of the mystic's selfish will and desires. This is the antonym of "abiding."

Enlightenment: *kashf*, and related terms, signify the drawing away of the veils of ignorance so that the light of spiritual truth may be revealed. This individual enlightenment, given by God, should not be confused with prophetic revelation, with which God reveals to His prophets their books and messages for guiding a community. Also see "inspiration," "revelation," and "veil."

Epiphany: *tajallī*, and related terms, signify God's presence revealed in creation and/or in the heart of His worshipper.

Essence: *dhāt*, the divine core of being.

Exhilaration: *basṭ*, and related terms, designate positive spiritual and emotional states of union encompassing the mystic and his/her surroundings. This is the antonym of "constriction."

Expansion: see "exhilaration."

Glory: ^{c}Ā'ishah uses several terms that mean glory and power, but one of them, *jalāl*, often designates one of God's attributes. God's discipline and wrath emanate from this attribute. *Jalāl* is the complement of *jamāl*, "beauty" and "splendor"

Gnosis: *^{c}arafah*, *^{c}irfān*, *dhawq*, and related terms, referring to a non-rational, experiential way of knowing the divine through the mystical experience. Also see "Islamic mysticism" and "mystical experience."

Ḥadīth: a report of the prophet Muhammad's sayings or actions, that is of his *sunnah* or "custom." The collected traditionally reliable reports are second only to the Qur'ān as a source of religious inspiration and law. Also see "Muhammad" and "Qur'ān.

Hajj: the "greater canonical pilgrimage," taking place in Mecca and its environs during the 8th -13th of Dhū al-Ḥijjah, the final month of the Muslim lunar calendar. Pilgrims undergo a ritual purification and wear a special garb while performing the specific prayers and rituals of the Hajj. Also see "Ka^{c}bah," "Mecca," "Medina," and "^{c}Umrah."

Hashimite: an epithet of the prophet Muhammad, referring to his clan of the Banū Hāshim within his tribe of the Quraysh. Also see "Muhammad."

Heart: ^{c}Ā'ishah uses several terms for the heart, including *qalb*, *fu'ād* and *sirr*, all of which refer to the seat of human emotion, especially love. For ^{c}Ā'ishah and many Sufis, the heart is also the site of divine inspiration and mystical experience. Also see "inspiration," "mystical experience," and "secret."

Imām: literally the "one in front;" in Sunni Islam, an imām is a prayer leader, and a title of respect.

Inspiration: *fatḥ*, *kashf*, and related terms, signifying God's gifts of mystical experience and spiritual enlightenment to an individual. Also see "enlightenment," "revelation," and "veil."

Intercession: *shafā^{c}ah*, and related terms, designate an individual's advocacy before God on behalf of those who worship Him in order to obtain His forgiveness of sins and a place for believers in Paradise. According to Muslim tradition, God has given the prophet Muhammad the power of intercession. Also see "Banner of Praise."

Intoxication: *sukr*, and related terms, signifying an overwhelming mystical state of love. Also see "wine."

Islamic Mysticism: *taṣawwuf*, also known as Sufism, designates the study of experiences within Islam characterized by ineffability, a sense of profundity, and transience, and frequently by a positive sense of passivity, timelessness, and unity. Islamic mysticism also includes the methods to attain and refine theses experiences, the theories and doctrines regarding their origin and significance, and the places of theses experiences within the lives of individuals and their societies. Also see: "audition," "gnosis," "heart," "mystical experience," and "recollection."

al-Jīlānī or al-Jīlī, ᶜAbd al-Qādir (d. 561/1166): progenitor of the Qādirīyah Sufi order to which ᶜĀ'ishah belonged. Born in Iran, al-Jīlānī spent much of his adult life preaching and teaching the Qur'ān, *ḥadīth*, law, and Islamic mysticism to disciples in Baghdad. In his teachings, al-Jīlānī stressed obedience to and love of God, the control of the selfish soul, and leading a moral life. Also see "*ḥadīth*," "Qur'ān," and "soul."

Jinn: singular: *jinnī*. In the Qur'ān, genies are a spiritual race and counterparts to humanity. In classical Arabic literature, when a genie possesses (*majnūn*) a human being, the genie may offer poetic inspiration, knowledge of unseen worlds, or drive the person mad.

Kaᶜbah: literally the cube, is the rectangular structure holding the black stone, which is the center of the Muslim pilgrimage. Also see "Hajj."

Lamp: *sirāj*, often a reference to the prophet Muhammad who brought guidance to humanity, hence the Qur'ān (33:46) calls him "a shining lamp" (*sirāj munīr*). Also see "Banner of Praise," "best of creation," and "best of humanity."

Mamluks: ruling dynasty of Egypt and greater Syria comprised of royal slave soldiers (singular: *mamlūk*) who succeeded their Ayyubid masters in 1250. The Mamluks were important to Islamic history both as patrons of the arts and defenders of the faith, as they stopped the Mongol hordes, who had wreaked havoc in other parts of the Muslim world. The Mamluk dynasty came to an end with their defeat by the Ottomans in 1516-17.

Marwah and Ṣafā: two small hills near the Kaᶜbah where pilgrims either walk or run as part of the Hajj and ᶜUmrah pilgrimages. Also see "Hajj" and "ᶜUmrah."

Mecca: the birth place of Muhammad in Arabia and site of the Kaᶜbah and the annual Hajj pilgrimage. Mecca is the most holy place on earth in Muslim tradition. Also see "Hajj," "Kaᶜbah," "Medina," and "Muhammad."

Medina: "city" of the Prophet, located about two hundred and fifty miles north of Mecca. Medina, formally known as Yathrib, became Muhammad's residence in 1/622 following the Muslim immigration (*hijrah*) from Mecca to Medina. The second holiest site in Muslim tradition, Medina is the location of Muhammad's tomb, which is often visited by pilgrims after the Hajj. Also see "Hajj," "Mecca," and "Muhammad."

Minā: a small oasis town on the Hajj pilgrimage route about three miles from Mecca where, according to tradition, Abraham sacrificed a ram in place of his son. Pilgrims cast stones at three pillars there that represent Satan's three attempts to dissuade Abraham's son from obeying his father, who intended to sacrifice him as God had ordered. Also see Hajj.

Muhammad: According to Muslim tradition, Muhammad was the final prophet sent by God to guide humanity to the straight path, to warn humans of the impending Day of Judgment, and to deliver the good news that God is compassionate and merciful. Muhammad was born in Mecca around 570 CE, and began to receive revelations around 610 CE, which continued until his death in Medina in 11/632. Also see "*ḥadīth*," "Hashamite," "Mecca," "Medina," and "Qur'ān."

Mystical Experience: psycho-somatic states characterized by ineffability, a profound quality, and transience, and frequently by a positive sense of receptivity, timelessness, and unity. Also see "gnosis" and "Islamic mysticism."

Nearness: *qurb*, and related terms, signify the mystic's closeness to God, and being in His presence. Also see "presence."

Passing Away: see "annihilation."

Power: *jalāl*: see "glory."

Presence: *ḥaḍrah*, and related terms, usually signify God's living and loving presence, whether in the world of nature, in the mystic's heart, or in the gardens of Paradise, where believers will contemplate God in the beatific vision. Also see "epiphany" and "nearness."

Proximity: see "nearness."

Qādirīyah: see "al-Jīlānī or al-Jīlī, ᶜAbd al-Qādir."

Qur'ān: the "recitation," the Muslim holy scripture consisting of 114 chapters of varying lengths from 3-286 verses. Probably collected after the death of the prophet Muhammad, the Qur'ān contains the revelations received by him between 610-632 CE. Also see "Muhammad."

Rapture: *wajd*, an Arabic word related to the term *wujūd*, which may mean both "existence" and "finding" God and/or ecstasy. *Wajd* designates a powerful emotional and spiritual state that often occurs during recollection and audition, and may result in feelings of grief due to separation from the beloved, or ecstatic joy in His presence. Also see "audition," "recollection," "separation," and "union."

Real: *al-Ḥaqq*, one of God's ninety-nine beautiful Names, which may also be translated as "The True."

Recollection: *dhikr*, the practice of remembering and meditating on God, often by using one of his Beautiful Names, or the profession of faith: "There is no deity but God, and Muhammad is the apostle of God." This practice may be part of Sufi audition rituals and may lead to mystical trance. Also see "audition."

Revelation: *kashf*, literally an "unveiling" of mystical and spiritual truth. It is a grace given by God to whom He wills. This enlightenment of an individual, although a great blessing, should not be confused with prophetic revelation, in which God reveals to His prophets their books and messages to guide a community. Also see "enlightenment," "inspiration" and "veil."

Ṣafā: see "Marwah."

Sāqī: the cup-bearer who serves wine.

Savior: *ghawth*, may be used of God, or it may signify an individual, such as ᶜĀ'ishah's spiritual master Jamāl al-Dīn Ismāᶜīl al-Ḥawwārī (d.900/1495), regarded as the greatest living saint or enlightened human being of a particular era. Also see "axis."

Secret: *sirr*, in classical Arabic poetry, the secret generally refers to the beloved's name and identity that are not to be revealed. In Sufism, the term *sirr* also designates the inner most center of the heart where God may appear to His loving worshipper. Also see "heart."

Separation: *ḥajr*, *ṣadd*, *biᶜād*, and related terms, signify the lover's distance from the beloved, usually due to some defect on the part of the lover who has yet to learn true selflessness. Also see "soul" and "union."

Sobriety: *ṣaḥw*, may allude to the mystic's unenlightened state prior to spiritual intoxication. However, "the second sobriety," may allude to a more stable enlightenment following an expansive intoxication.

Soul: *nafs*, the "self" in "selfishness." In Islam, the selfish soul is not an immortal principle within the human being. Rather, it is equivalent to concupiscence, which tends toward immediate gratification of appetites, no matter the cost. In Sufism, the selfish soul is to be disciplined and controlled, often by fasting, seclusion, and mental vigilance.

Spirit: *rūḥ*, an element of the divine within each human being. Qu'rān 32:9 states that God "fashioned [Adam] and breathed into him with His spirit (*rūḥ*)." For ᶜĀ'ishah, and other Sufis, this event underscores the close loving relationship between God and the human being, and it is through recollection that a mystic's spirit may temporally return to the divine presence, prior to the Judgment Day. Also see "recollection" and "audition."

Splendor: *jamāl*: see "beauty."

Spout of His Blessings: *mīzāb al-faḍlihi* or, more commonly, *mīzāb al-raḥmah*, the "waterspout of mercy," is located at the top of the northwest wall of the Kaᶜbah and is regarded as a source of God's mercy and blessings. Also see "Kaᶜbah."

State: *ḥāl*, *ḥālah*, a transient mystical state or condition given by God to His worshipper. States include contraction, expansion, intoxication, annihilation, and abiding. Also see "abiding," "annihilation," "contraction," "expansion," "intoxication," and "station."

Station: *maqām*, *manzil*, a worshipper's spiritual level attained through study, discipline and religious fortitude, and often assisted by various mystical states sent by God. Whereas states are transient, the station is more stable. Sufis posit a number of stations in their mystical itineraries, which may include repentance, poverty, trust in God, love, annihilation, and abiding. Also see "abiding," "annihilation," and "state."

Sufi: a Muslim mystic.

Sufism: see "Islamic Mysticism."

True: *al-Ḥaqq*, is one of God's ninety-nine beautiful Names, which may also be translated as "The Real."

ᶜUmrah: the "lesser pilgrimage" whose rites and rituals at the sacred precinct in Mecca may be done at any time by a believer, in contrast to the Hajj. Also see "Hajj" and "Marwah."

Union: ^{c}Ā'ishah uses several terms for union, but most often *waṣl*, *wiṣāl*, and *jam^{c}*. For ^{c}Ā'ishah, union is not the mingling of two substances together, but the annihilation of the selfish soul in love of God, the One, the Real, Who, by an act of grace, draws His worsipper near to abide in His loving presence. Also see "separation."

Veil: *ḥijāb*, plural: *ḥujub*, usually alludes to spiritual ignorance, or the inability to see the divine nature within (*bāṭin*) external forms (*ẓāhir*). Also see "enlightenment," "inspiration" and "revelation."

Wine: a major theme in the verse of ^{c}Ā'ishah al-Bā^{c}ūnīyah, and a metaphor for God's intoxicating love and the future bliss of Paradise. Also see "intoxication."

Zamzam: the well located near the Ka^{c}bah, whose water is a source of great blessings.

Bibliography

Abū Nuwās, *Dīwān*. Edited by Ewald Wagner. 4 vols. Wiesbaden, 1988.

^{c}Ā'ishah al-Bā^{c}ūnīyah. *Dīwān ^{c}Ā'ishah al-Bā^{c}ūnīyah* (= *Fayḍ al-Faḍl*). Microfilm 29322 of MS 431 (Shi^{c}r Taymūr). MS 581 (Shi^{c}r Taymūr). MS 4384 (Adab). Cairo: Dār al-Kutub al-Miṣrīyah. MS 734, Rabat: Bibliothèque Generale.

———. *Dīwān Fayḍ al-Faḍl wa-Jam ^{c} al-Shaml*, edited by Mahdi As'ad ^{c}Arrar. Beirut: Dār al-Kutub al-^{c}Ilmīyah, 2010.

———. *Al-Muntakhab fī Uṣūl al-Rutab fī ^{c}Ilm al-Taṣawwuf.* Microfilm 13123 of MS 318 (Taṣawwuf Taymūr). Cairo: Dār al-Kutub al-Miṣrīyah.

———. *Al-Mawrid al-Ahnā fī al-Mawlid al-Asnā.* MS 639 (Shi^{c}r Taymūr). Cairo: Dār al-Kutub al-Miṣrīyah.

al-^{c}Alāwī, Fāris Aḥmad. *^{c}Ā'ishah al-Bā^{c}ūnīyah al-Dimashqīyah.* Damascus, 1994.

Berkey, Jonathan P. "Women and Islamic Education in the Mamluk Period." In *Women in Middle Eastern History*. Edited by Nikki R. Keddie and Beth Baron. New Haven, 1991, 143-57.

Bly, Robert. *The Eight Stages of Translation.* Boston, 1983.

Bonebakker, S. A. *Some Early Definitions of the Tawryia and Safadī's Fadd al-Xitām ^{c}an at-Tawrīya wa'l-Istixdām* (The Hague, 1966).

al-Būrīnī, al-Ḥasan. *Sharḥ Dīwān Sulṭān al-Āshiqīn Sayyidī ^{c}Umar Ibn al-Fāriḍ.* Edited by Rushayyid ibn Ghālib al-Daḥdāḥ. 2 vols. in 1. Cairo, 1888.

Chittick, William C. *The Sufi Path of Knowledge.* Albany, 1989.

al-Dhahabī, Mājid and Salāḥ al-Khiyamī. "Dīwān ^{c}Ā'ishah al-Bā^{c}ūnīyah." *Turāth al-^{c}Arabī* 4 (1981):110-121. Damascus.

During, Jean. *Musique et extase.* Paris, 1988.

al-Ghazzī, Najm al-Dīn Muhammad. *Al-Kawākib al-Sā'irah.* Edited by Jibrā'īl Sulaymān Jabbūr. 3 vols. Beirut, 1945.

Gibb, H.A.R., et.al., eds. *Encyclopaedia of Islam.* 2nd ed. 11 vols. in 14. Leiden, 1954-2009.

Homerin, Th. Emil. "ᶜĀ'ishah al-Bāᶜūnīyah (d. 1517)." In *Essays in Arabic Literary Biography II: 1350-1850*. Editied by Devin Stewart and Joseph Lowry. Wiesbaden, 2010, 21-27.

———. *From Arab Poet to Muslim Saint: Ibn al-Fāriḍ, His Verse, and His Shrine*, 2nd ed. Cairo, 2001.

———. "Ibn al-Fāriḍ's Personal *Dīwān*." *In Le développement du Soufisme en Égypte à l'èpoque mamelouke*. Edited by Richard McGregor and Adam Sabra. Cairo, 2006, 233-43.

———. "Living Love: The Mystical Writings of ᶜĀ'ishah al-Bāᶜūnīyah." *Mamlūk Studies Review* 7:1 (2003): 211-36.

———. *ᶜUmar Ibn al-Fāriḍ: Sufi Verse, Saintly Life*. New York, 2001.

———. *The Wine of Love and Life: Ibn Fāriḍ's al-Khamrīah and al-Qayṣarī's Quest for Meaning*. Chicago, 2005.

———. "Writing Sufi Biography: The Case of ᶜĀ'ishah al-Bāᶜūnīyah (d. 923/1517)." *Muslim World* 96:3 (2006): 389-99.

Ibn al-Fāriḍ, ᶜUmar. *Dīwān Ibn al-Fāriḍ*. Ed. Guiseppe Scattolin. Cairo, 2004.

Ibn al-Ḥanbalī al-Ḥalabī, *Durr al-Ḥabab fī Ta'rīkh Aᶜyān Ḥalab*. Edited by Maḥmūd al-Fākhūrī and Yaḥyā ᶜAbbārah. Damascus, 1973.

Ibn al-ᶜImād, ᶜAbd al-Ḥayy. *Shadharāt al-Dhahab fī Akhbār Man Dhahab*. 12 vols in 6. Cairo, 1931.

Ibn Isḥāq, *The Life of Muhammad*. Translated by A. Guillaume. Oxford, 1955.

Ibn Mullā al-Ḥaṣkafī, *Mutᶜat al-Adhān Min al-Tamattuᶜ bi-al-Iqrān*. Edited by Ṣalāḥ al-Dīn Khalīl al-Shaybānī al-Mawṣilī. 2 vols. Beirut, 1999.

Ibn Ṭūlūn, Muhammad. *Mufākahat al-Khillān fī Ḥawādith al-Zamān*. Edited by M. Muṣtafā. 2 vols. Cairo, 1962-64.

———. *al-Qalā'id al-Jawharīyah fī Ta'īkh a-Ṣāliḥīyah*. Editied by Muhammad Aḥmad Duhmān. 2 vols. Damascus, 1980.

Kennedy, Philip F. *Abu Nuwas: A Genius of Poetry*. Oxford, 2005.

Knysh, Alexander. *Islamic Mysticism: A Short Introduction*. Leiden, 2000.

Lamoreaux, John C. *The Early Muslim Tradition of Dream Interpretation*. Albany, 2002.

Lutfi, Huda. "Al-Sakhawī's *Kitāb al-Nisā'* as a Source for the Social and Economic History of Muslim Women during the Fifteenth Century A.D." *Muslim World* 71(1981):104-24.

Meir, Fritz. "The Dervish Dance: An Attempt at an Overview." In *Essays on Islamic Piety and Mysticism*. Translated by John O'Kane. Leiden, 1999, 23-48.

Meri, Josef W. *The Cult of the Saints Among Muslims and Jews in Medieval Syria*. Oxford, 2002.

Meisami, Julie Scott and Paul Starkey, eds. *Encyclopedia of Arabic Literature*. 2 vols. London, 1998.

Mukhliṣ, ᶜAbd Allāh. "ᶜĀ'ishah al-Bāᶜūnīyah." *Mujallat al-Majmaᶜ al-ᶜIlmī* 16:2:66-72. Damascus, 1941.

Petry, Carl. *Twilight of Majesty*. Seattle, 1993.

al-Qadḥāt, Muhammad ᶜAbd Allāh. *ᶜĀ'ilat al-Bāᶜūnī*. Amman, 2007.

al-Qushayrī, Abū al-Qāsim. *Al-Qushayri's Epistle on Sufism*. Translated by Alexander Knysh. Reading, UK, 2007.

Rabābiᶜah, Ḥasan. *ᶜĀ'ishah al-Bāᶜūnīyah: Shāᶜirah*. Irbid, Jordan, 1997.

Schimmel, Annemarie. *And Muhammad Is His Messenger*. Chapel Hill, NC, 1985.

———. *Mystical Dimensions* of Islam. Chapel Hill, NC, 1975

Von Grunebaum, G.E. *Muhammadan Festivals*. New York, 1951.